AFRICAN-AMERICAN WRITERS

MULTICULTURAL VOICES

AFRICAN-AMERICAN WRITERS

ARAB-AMERICAN AND MUSLIM WRITERS

ASIAN-AMERICAN WRITERS

HISPANIC-AMERICAN WRITERS

NATIVE AMERICAN WRITERS

MULTICULTURAL VOICES

AFRICAN-AMERICAN WRITERS

AMY SICKELS

CHELSEA HOUSE
PUBLISHERS
An imprint of Infobase Publishing

MULTICULTURAL VOICES: African-American Writers

Copyright © 2010 by Infobase Publishing

Chelsea House
An imprint of Infobase Publishing
132 West 31st Street
New York NY 10001

Library of Congress Cataloging-in-Publication Data
Sickels, Amy.
  African-American writers / Amy Sickels.
    p. cm. — (Multicultural voices)
Includes bibliographical references and index.
ISBN 978-1-60413-311-0 (hardcover)
  1. American literature—African American authors—Juvenile literature. 2. African American authors—Biography—Juvenile literature. 3. African Americans in literature—Juvenile literature. 4. African Americans—Intellectual life—Juvenile literature. I. Title.
PS153.N5S54 2010
810.9'896073—dc22
[B]   2009037856

Chelsea House books are available at special discounts when purchased in bulk quantities for businesses, associations, institutions, or sales promotions. Please call our Special Sales Department in New York at (212) 967-8800 or (800) 322-8755.

You can find Chelsea House on the World Wide Web at
http://www.chelseahouse.com

Text design and composition by Lina Farinella
Cover design by Alicia Post
Cover printed by IBT Global, Inc., Troy NY
Book printed and bound by IBT Global, Inc., Troy NY
Date printed: February 2010

Printed in the United States of America

10 9 8 7 6 5 4 3 2 1

This book is printed on acid-free paper.

All links and Web addresses were checked and verified to be correct at the time of publication. Because of the dynamic nature of the Web, some addresses and links may have changed since publication and may no longer be valid.

CONTENTS

OVERVIEW

THE DEEP-ROOTED TRADITION of African-American literature traces its origin to the earliest days of the nation's history. Poetry and oral and slave narratives recorded voices of struggle and triumph and gave rise to the rich and diverse array of writing that has characterized the twentieth century and beyond. The Harlem Renaissance and the civil rights and Black Arts movements played significant, dynamic roles in the shaping and development of African-American literature. Today, African-American writing continues to build on and redefine the foundation of literature in the United States, with the work of such prominent authors as Toni Morrison, Maya Angelou, and Ernest Gaines, among many others, securing a popular and diverse audience and inspiring a large output of critical scholarship.

The development of an African-American literature began more than 200 years ago. The first published African-American poet was Phillis Wheatley, a slave whose book of poems appeared in 1784. Throughout the eighteenth and nineteenth centuries, before the Civil War, slave narratives also emerged as a popular form of protest literature. Though white abolitionists often penned slave narratives for political purposes, many former slaves, including Harriet Jacobs and Frederick Douglass, among thousands of others, also wrote slave narratives about their personal experiences. After the Civil War, the abolition of slavery, and the onset of the Reconstruction era, several well-known black writers and activists, including W.E.B Du Bois, Booker T. Washington, and Marcus Garvey, wrote about the conditions of black lives in America, their work changing and correcting social and cultural understandings of race. The first African-American poet to gain popularity and critical reception was Paul Laurence Dunbar, whose first book of poetry, *Oak and Ivy* (1893), describes the lives of rural African Americans.

In the 1920s and early 1930s, Harlem, in New York City, became a mecca for African-American artists, writers, intellectuals, and musicians, and the movement that assembled around them became known as the Harlem Renaissance. This was a time when the country was steeped in Jim Crow laws and the racist ideologies they enforced, and many southern blacks migrated to the North for employment as well as to escape oppression and violence. Hope for the future and belief in the need for change were reflected in the arts. Between 1919 and 1930, black authors were published in greater numbers than any other decade before the 1960s. Langston Hughes, Zora Neale Hurston, Jean Toomer, and Countee Cullen were all important writers of the Harlem Renaissance. Slowly, African-American literature, music, and other arts began to gain a wider appeal and audience; despite this increasing exposure, African-American literature was still many years away from being recognized by academic scholarship or the popular literary world.

In the years following the heyday of the Harlem Renaissance, many African Americans continued migrating from the rural South, the flow hitting a high point during World War II. Mostly people gravitated to industrial centers and, in particular, cities such as New York, Chicago, and Detroit, where the new arrivals often found factory work. The migration contributed to a more vibrant, urban black community and culture and helped to lay the groundwork for the civil rights movement. For the first time, dominant white society began to take notice and pay close attention to the African-American voices adding to and challenging the dominant, mainstream culture. Richard Wright's novel *Native Son* (1940), which protested the social conditions that white society imposed on African Americans, became an immediate best-seller and was selected for the Book-of-the-Month Club. Its success helped to establish Wright as a spokesman for African-American issues. In 1949, Gwendolyn Brooks became the first African American to win the Pulitzer Prize, awarded for her book of poems *Annie Allen*. Ralph Ellison won the National Book Award in 1953 for his novel *Invisible Man*, which addresses social conditions, post–Civil War black identity, and universal themes of humanity and justice. For the first time, African-American authors were getting the attention their works deserved, winning awards and receiving honors that for so long had been reserved only for white writers.

The 1950s and 1960s were among the most politically explosive times in modern American history, as the civil rights movement rose up against the segregation, violence, and racism that dominated the American South. Change began to ripple across the country, one significant shift coming with the Supreme Court ruling in *Brown v. Board of Education* (1954), which outlawed school segregation. The court's decision eventually led to the admission of large numbers of African-American students to public schools and eventually universities. Though many universities considered themselves open to new ideas and increasingly diverse voices, many employed segregationist policies and resisted the enrollment of African-American students. Several reputable black colleges around the country, including Howard University, Fisk College, and Spelman College, drew talented and diverse students, but many public and private colleges, including the schools that make up the Ivy League, accepted none or very few African-American students.

As a result, scholarship on African-American literature remained nonexistent in mainstream universities; African-American literature was predominately absent from the curriculum at most academic institutions and would remain in isolation until the 1970s.

Since the earliest days of the African-American literary tradition in the United States, politics, social conditions, and culture have been entwined in its creation. During the civil rights movement, many black writers used their fiction, poetry, and nonfiction to fuel the growing social protest. As black activists fought to end segregation and secure civil rights, black authors addressed these issues in their work. One major writer who began publishing in the 1950s and wrote throughout the 1970s was James Baldwin, a gay man whose work addressed both race and sexuality. He wrote nearly 20 works of fiction and nonfiction, including *Go Tell It on the Mountain, Another Country*, and *The Fire Next Time*. As Baldwin became more active in the growing civil rights movement, with eloquent essays such as "Down at the Cross," he quickly captured the attention of the American public. When Baldwin's collection of essays *Nobody Knows My Name* was published in 1961, it remained on the best-seller list for six months. Baldwin's writing illustrated the danger of a divided America and challenged both whites and blacks to reach out to one another. Baldwin's success, as well as the growing popularity of other African-American writers, actors, and musicians, revealed that much of white society wanted to learn more about African-American life and culture and to find ways of crossing society's rigid divides.

Another example of a black artist finding mainstream success was Lorraine Hansberry, whose play *A Raisin in the Sun* became a Broadway hit in 1959. Hansberry was the first African-American woman to have a play on Broadway and the youngest and first African American to win the New York Drama Critics' Circle Award. Also in the 1950s, the Harlem Writers Guild, the oldest organization of African-American writers in the United States, was created and served as an early advocate for the development of black literature. Many well-known writers over the years were a part of the organization, including Audre Lorde, Paule Marshall, Lorraine Hansberry, Terry McMillan, and Walter Dean Myers.

The strong connection between writing and activism deepened, as symbolized by Martin Luther King Jr.'s famous and eloquent "Letter from a Birmingham Jail." Many prominent writers and civil rights leaders joined forces, adding eloquence to action. Maya Angelou, for instance, was a close friend of King's and, in 1959, became the northern coordinator for the Southern Christian Leadership Conference. Later, when she was living in Africa, Angelou also became close friends with the activist Malcolm X and helped him build a new civil rights organization, the Organization of African American Unity. Malcolm X, a leader of black Muslims, became known throughout the United States as a fiery advocate for black unity and militancy. He distanced himself from other civil rights leaders, such as King, who advocated peaceful resistance. When Malcolm X's autobiography, written by

Alex Haley, was published after his death, it was regarded as an important piece of literature about race in the United States and a powerful portrayal of one man's personal and spiritual transformation.

The writer Alice Walker was also active in the civil rights movement, involved with voter registration drives, campaigns for welfare rights, and children's programs. Gwendolyn Brooks, Nikki Giovanni, and Sonia Sanchez wrote poems about justice and equality, their work contributing to the civil rights and Black Power movements. This idea of African-American literature as a tool for activism was not new—from the slave narratives to the fiction of Richard Wright, African-American literature was often used as a way to promote political and cultural liberation.

As the civil rights movement gained momentum, it also came under vicious attack, with church bombings and lynchings claiming the lives of African Americans. Malcolm X, whose views had tempered somewhat to be more accepting of whites, was assassinated. This period also marked the early years of the Vietnam War, which would incite protests, controversy, and turbulence. The hope for change and the drive for equality continued to gain force, nonetheless, with the momentous March on Washington in 1963 helping to lead to the passing of the most important pieces of legislation of the 1960s: the Civil Rights Act of 1964 and the Voting Rights Act of 1965.

The deep connection between art and politics continued to inform and influence the rest of the 1960s and 1970s, as black artists and intellectuals began to focus on black unity and solidarity. The Black Arts movement, the cultural wing of the Black Power movement that was started by the poet Amiri Baraka in 1965, was influential in the work and development of many writers. The movement helped to form black publishing houses, theater troupes, and poetry readings. African Americans began to openly celebrate and incorporate into their lives and art the songs, stories, and customs of ancestors in a renewed effort to examine and affirm their connection to Africa and the cultural past. Poetry became a political weapon, as demonstrated by Amiri Baraka, Nikki Giovanni, and Gwendolyn Brooks. Playwright August Wilson also wrote poetry and was involved in the Black Power moment, in addition to co-founding the Black Horizon Theater in the Hill District of Pittsburgh. The writer Charles Johnson, also a prominent figure in the Black Arts movement, first received attention as a political cartoonist. While much of the Black Power movement was shaped by a male perspective, women writers such as June Jordan, Lucille Clifton, and Audre Lorde also made their voices heard at this time, by writing about sexism and homophobia.

When Martin Luther King Jr. was assassinated on April 4, 1968, the nation was stunned, saddened, and angered, and the killing set off a series of riots across the country. Maya Angelou was deeply depressed by her friend's murder, meeting with James Baldwin and other friends, who encouraged her to write her autobiography as a way to address and dispel her mourning; eventually, this led to her acclaimed work *I Know Why the Caged Bird Sings*. Others around the country also put aside their grief and continued with the struggle for justice and equal rights. The momentum of the civil rights movement inspired other causes and groups, including the women's movement and the gay and lesbian rights movement.

In the 1970s, with the Black Power movement starting to decline, African-American literature started to focus on more specific issues within the community. This was a critical decade for African-American literature, as it began to gain a wider readership and, for the first time, to be defined as a genre and recognized as a crucial part of the larger category of American literature. Two anthologies that appeared in the late 1960s and were significant in defining African-American literature were *Dark Symphony: Negro Literature in America* (1968), edited by James Emanuel and Theodore Gross, and *Black Fire: An Anthology of Afro-American Writing* (1968), edited by Amiri Baraka and Larry Neal. In addition, as an editor at Random House, Toni Morrison specialized in publishing and editing black writers, helping to launch the careers of Angela Davis, Toni Cade Bambara, and Gayle Jones. The identity of a distinctly African-American literature began to emerge more definitively, as more black authors published critically acclaimed works.

The Civil Rights Act and Black Power movement paved the way for a small number of African Americans to enter historically white universities, including Harvard, Cornell, Princeton, Yale, and Columbia. This representation of African Americans in the academy, as both faculty and students, challenged the racism that existed in these institutions and eventually changed the study of American literature to include African-American writings. It was not an easy implementation, but African-American scholars persevered and began to develop African-American studies programs and departments. Works by African-American writers began to slowly be accepted by the academy as a legitimate and necessary part of American literature.

The 1970s were an especially vital and fruitful period for black women writers, helping to lay the foundation for literary scholarship on black women authors of the past as well as to develop the ideas central to black feminist criticism. The small but significant number of African-American women in primarily white universities began to challenge the absence of their own histories in academia and began the important excavation of long-forgotten black women's history and literature. Alice Walker's seminal 1974 essay, "The Search for Zora Neale Hurston," was largely responsible for the renewal of interest in the work of the writer whose novel *Their Eyes Were Watching God* had been neglected after its brief success during the Harlem Renaissance. Walker, who as a black feminist considers herself a "womanist," also reclaimed the legacy of other southern black women by focusing on their art forms—such as gardening and quilting—in her book *In Search of Our Mothers' Gardens*. Another work that gained widespread recognition after it was reprinted was *Brown Girl, Brownstones* by Paule Marshall. Originally published in 1959, the novel describes the lives of Barbadian immigrants in Brooklyn during the Great Depression and World War II; until it was republished in 1981, it had virtually disappeared from American literature.

While rediscovering some of the overlooked or forgotten voices of the past, African-American women writers continued to produce vital work of their own, garnering popular and critical accolades. The anthology *The Black Women*, edited by Toni Cade Bambara, and first novels by Alice Walker, June Jordan, and Toni Morrison were all published in 1970. Maya Angelou's *I Know Why the Caged Bird Sings* won popular and critical acclaim and was nominated for the National Book Award. The following year, Angelou's book of poetry *Just Give Me A Cool Drink of Water 'Fore I Diiie* received a Pulitzer Prize nomination. In 1975, Ntozake Shange's choreographed poem *for colored girls who have considered suicide / when the rainbow is enuf* was produced on Broadway to great success, while stirring up debates in the African-American community about sexism. Alice Walker's *The Color Purple* became a best-seller and received the National Book Award in 1983. She was also the first African-American woman to be awarded the Pulitzer Prize for fiction. The novel also touched off controversy among critics and black scholars, who accused Walker of negatively portraying black men. Walker's novel simply took its place among a growing number of works that analyzed the complexities underlying African-American culture and history, protested the sexism within the black community, and demonstrated how black communities had internalized racist stereotypes. Toni Morrison wrote *The Bluest Eye*, partially influenced by the growing effort to reclaim African-American beauty as summarized and expressed in the motto and rallying cry "Black Is Beautiful." By telling the story of one little girl's desire for love, Morrison reveals the broken dreams and self-hatred that could infect and harm an entire community. African-American women writers expanded and enriched the nation's literature, providing incisive explorations of themes including gender issues, motherhood, mother/daughter relationships, women's friendship, sexuality, and spirituality.

The last decades of the twentieth century also witnessed an explosion of children's and young adult books penned by African-American writers. The poet Lucille Clifton published many books for children, and Rosa Guy wrote a trilogy for young adults that focused on two Harlem families and an adolescent's coming of age. Starting in the early 1980s, Joyce Carol Thomas wrote many children's and young adult books about black life in Oklahoma and on the West Coast. Until then, juvenile publishers had contracted very few books featuring African-American characters. Starting in the mid-1970s, and gaining momentum in the ensuing decades, publishers released books that depicted realistic, complex, and positive portrayals of young African Americans. Some of these books included Walter Dean Myers's *Fast Sam, Cool Clyde, and Stuff*; June Jordan's *His Own Where*; Alice Childress's *A Hero Ain't Nothin' but a Sandwich*; and Kristin Hunter's *The Soul Brothers and Sister Lou*.

The majority of African-American writers who grew up before the 1980s did not have access to a variety of books about African Americans. Schools simply did not teach works by African-American writers. Walter Dean Myers grew up reading only the English and white American authors who were assigned in school; though he lived in Harlem, Myers was only faintly aware of the rich history of the Harlem Renaissance. Maya Angelou also grew up reading only white authors, until one day she encountered the poetry of James Weldon Johnson, a moment that deeply impacted her. On the other hand, August Wilson, who grew up in Pittsburgh, dropped out of school (where work by black authors was not taught) and educated himself at the Carnegie Library, reading many black writers including Ralph Ellison, Richard Wright, and Langston Hughes. Gloria Naylor was in college when she read her first novel by an African-American woman: Toni Morrison's *The Bluest Eye*, which gave her the inspiration to produce work of her own.

While much African-American writing of the 1950s and 1960s considered slavery to be a degrading part of the past and rarely focused on this history, throughout the mid-1970s to the current day, African-American writers began to look at the slavery era as a way to understand the present. Novels such as Ernest J. Gaines's *The Autobiography of Miss Jane Pittman*, Charles Johnson's *Middle Passage*, and Toni Morrison's *Beloved* all take slavery or its wide-reaching legacy as their central subjects. African-American writers challenged themselves to find new ways to return to the past in order to find greater meaning and insight in the present. Onstage, August Wilson saw theater as a way to raise the collective consciousness about black life in the United States, committing himself to writing a cycle of 10 plays that would revisit the concerns and issues informing each decade of the twentieth century.

The influence of African ancestry is also apparent in the work of many writers, including Alice Walker, Ishmael Reed, Charles Johnson, Toni Morrison, and August Wilson. African legacy and spirituality, the oppression of colonialism and imperialism, and the connection of modern-day African Americans to their African ancestors are just a few of the themes explored. Writers also examined traditional forms of storytelling and African-American forms of expression, including music and folklore. Walker's *The Color Purple*, for example, which uses a first-person narrator to describe the life of an uneducated, oppressed woman, inspired scholarly interest in black English and dialect. Ernest Gaines uses the oral storytelling form to structure *The Autobiography of Miss Jane Pittman*, while August Wilson employs musical forms in his work to portray African-American roots and nonverbal forms of communication.

Though African-American writers were becoming well known in the popular and literary realm, black critics were largely absent. By the mid-1980s, however, literary theory was crucial in developing the study of black literature, with prominent critics including Robert Stepto, Barbara Christian, Michael Harper, and Henry Louis Gates Jr. publishing influential books. African-American studies also gained prominence as an area of scholarship, in turn influencing the development of cultural studies (which focuses on political, economic, and social factors), cultural anthropology, and literary theory, among other areas, to explore cultural phenomena in various societies. Prominent African-American cultural critics, some of whom are popularly known in their role as public intellectuals, include Cornel West, Ishmael Reed, bell hooks, Michele Wallace, and Shelby Steele. Similarly, the 1980s also witnessed the emergence of multicultural education, which surfaced as a way to challenge Eurocentric bias in schools and expose students to a broader range of subjects and ideas. Intellectual and social movements were the driving factors in this major change implemented in schools across the country, though the roots of multicultural education can be traced back to the civil rights movement.

Not only does substantial scholarship on African-American literature now exist, but the presence of African-American writers in popular culture continues to grow exponentially. In 1992, three books by African-American writers would appear simultaneously on the *New York Times* best-seller list: *Waiting to Exhale* by Terry McMillan, *Jazz* by Toni Morrison, and *Possessing the Secret of Joy* by Alice Walker. In 1993, Maya Angelou recited her poem "On the Pulse of Morning" at President Bill Clinton's inauguration, the first poet to read an inaugural poem since Robert Frost at John F. Kennedy's inauguration in 1961. That same year, Rita Dove was named poet laureate. Also in 1993, Toni Morrison became the first African American to be awarded the prestigious Nobel Prize in Literature, her writing earning the respect and admiration of the international literary community.

Throughout the 1990s and into the twenty-first century, the long list of critically acclaimed and popular African-American authors continues to grow and diversify. Other prominent authors who emerged include fiction writers Jamaica Kincaid, Ishmael Reed, Randall Kenan, and John Edgar Wideman; poets Yusef Komunyakaa, Michael Harper, Carl Phillips, and Natasha Trethewey; and playwrights Ntozake Shange, Suzan-Lori Parks, and Lynn Nottage. Novelist Edward Jones recently won the Pulitzer Prize for fiction in 2004 for *The Known World*, a novel about a black slaveholder in the antebellum South. Younger novelists such as Edwidge Danticat, ZZ Packer, and Colson Whitehead are also making valuable contributions to the tradition and development of African-American literature.

The themes and subjects found in African-American literature have expanded widely, and today more than ever it is nearly impossible to group the work of African-American authors under a single heading. Cultural, social, and political ideas continue to change and become entwined. Colson Whitehead's novel *The Intuitionist* (1998), for example, blends aspects of other genres to explore race, technology, and the imagination; and in his collection of short stories, *Let the Dead Bury Their Dead* (1993), Randall Kenan often explores the psyches of white characters. African-American authors have also found success by writing in different genres, which has helped expand the definition of literature. Chester Hines was an early groundbreaker with his 1950s and 1960s pulp-fiction detective novels; Walter Mosley, who writes detective novels, is now one of the country's best-known novelists. Esteemed African-American authors who have contributed to the area of science fiction and fantasy include Samuel Delany and Octavia Butler. Terri McMillan shattered publishers' false ideas about the reading habits of African Americans when her 1992 novel, *Waiting to Exhale*, remained on the *New York Times* best-seller list for 24 weeks. As a result of such commercial success, editors at major publishing houses wanted to publish more African-American writers, realizing that there was a large audience of readers who had been neglected for too long. Another popular writer was E. Lynn Harris, an author known for his novels typically about closeted gay black men. His predominant audience is made up of black straight women, but his work also crosses over to gay and white audiences.

African-American literature occupies a central and abiding place in the nation's schools, colleges, and universities; the story of the nation's literature is indistinguishable from the contributions African Americans have made to it. The United States is a rich tapestry of religious, ethnic, racial, and cultural diversity, and American literature reflects this diversity, encouraging multiple backgrounds and perspectives and expanding the borders of the canon to include the broadest possible range of authors and voices. African-American literature has helped to recast the perception of what valuable and lasting literature is, forcing a reevaluation of the national literature. More democratic in principal, American literature has evolved, emerging as a changing, ever-expanding entity that is open to writers of various social, economic, and racially diverse backgrounds.

Similar to jazz and hip-hop, African-American literature began within the black community but now reaches a large, diverse, international audience and contributes to the revitalization and expansion of American culture. The select authors profiled in this volume are frequently taught in high schools around the country. The books discussed were all published within the last 40 years, and each continues to resonate with readers today. These diverse and influential works are just a few of the invaluable literary offerings African Americans have added and will continue to contribute, a vital and enduring part of American literature today.

MAYA ANGELOU

Biography

MAYA ANGELOU was born Marguerite Johnson in St. Louis, Missouri, on April 4, 1928, to Bailey Johnson and Vivian Baxter Johnson. When Angelou was three and her brother four, their parents divorced and sent the children alone by train to live with their grandmother in Stamps, Arkansas. When Maya was 13, she and her brother returned to live with their mother in San Francisco, California; during World War II, Angelou attended George Washington High School and studied dance and drama on a scholarship at the California Labor School. Before graduating, she worked as the first black female streetcar conductor in San Francisco. Three weeks after completing school, Angelou, at the age of 16, gave birth to her son, Clyde. She writes about these events and the first 17 years of her life in her first book, *I Know Why the Caged Bird Sings* (1970).

After a brief marriage to sailor Tosh Angelos, Angelou began dancing at the Purple Onion, a San Francisco nightclub, and toured Europe with a production of the opera *Porgy and Bess* in 1954–1955. She studied modern dance with Martha Graham and recorded her first record album, *Miss Calypso*, in 1957. At the end of the 1950s, Angelou moved to New York City, where she acted in off-Broadway productions and met artists and writers active in the civil rights movement.

In 1959, at the request of Martin Luther King Jr., Maya Angelou became the northern coordinator for the Southern Christian Leadership Conference. From 1961 to 1962, she was associate editor of *The Arab Observer* in Cairo, Egypt, the only English-language news weekly in the Middle East. When she and her son moved to Ghana, she became an assistant administrator at the University of Ghana's School of Music and Drama and a feature editor for *The African Review*. Angelou became close friends with Malcolm X and returned to the United States in

1964 to help him build a new civil rights organization, the Organization of African American Unity.

Martin Luther King's assassination on Angelou's birthday, April 4, 1968, left her deeply depressed. She met with her friends James Baldwin, cartoonist Jules Feiffer, and Feiffer's wife, Judy, who encouraged her to write her autobiography. When *I Know Why the Caged Bird Sings* was published in 1970, the book won popular and critical acclaim and was nominated for the National Book Award. The following year her book of poetry *Just Give Me A Cool Drink of Water 'Fore I Diiie* (1971) received a Pulitzer Prize nomination.

In 1973, Angelou married Paul du Feu and moved to Sonoma, California. During these years, she composed music for movies and songs for Roberta Flack, wrote for television, and wrote articles, short stories, poetry, and autobiographies. She appeared in a supporting role in the television miniseries *Roots* in 1977. Her screenplay, *Georgia, Georgia*, was the first original script by a black woman to be produced. It was also during this time that Angelou met Oprah Winfrey and became her mentor.

Angelou divorced in 1978. In 1981, she was appointed to the first lifetime Reynolds Professorship of American Studies at Wake Forest University in Winston-Salem, North Carolina. In 1993, she recited her poem "On the Pulse of Morning" at President Bill Clinton's inauguration, the first poet to give an inaugural reading since Robert Frost at John F. Kennedy's inauguration in 1961. In 1993, Angelou's poems were featured in the Janet Jackson/John Singleton film *Poetic Justice*. Angelou has also won three Grammys for her spoken-word albums. She has been awarded more than 30 honorary degrees and, in 2000, was awarded the Presidential Medal of Arts. In 2006, Angelou became a radio talk-show host for the first time on a weekly show for XM Satellite Radio's Oprah & Friends channel.

Author, poet, playwright, dancer, stage and screen producer, director, and civil rights activist, Maya Angelou is best known for her autobiographies and poetry. After the publication of *I Know Why the Caged Bird Sings*, Angelou published six more autobiographies, including *The Heart of a Woman* (1981) and *All God's Children Need Traveling Shoes* (1986). She has also published many volumes of poetry such as *Oh Pray My Wings Are Gonna Fit Me Well* (1975) and *I Shall Not Be Moved* (1990), as well as volumes of essays including *Wouldn't Take Nothing for My Journey Now* (1993). *I Know Why the Caged Bird Sings* continues to be her most popular and critically acclaimed work. In 1995, Bantam Books recognized her for having the longest-running appearance on the *New York Times* paperback nonfiction best-seller list. The book has also been the frequent target of censors and appears on the American Library Association list of the 100 Most Frequently Challenged Books.

One of the major themes that emerges in Angelou's work is the hope for freedom in the midst of oppression, as symbolized by the caged bird that can only raise its voice in protest. Her writing depicts the realities of racism and the ways the African-American community has resisted and overcome oppression. Hope, strength, and compassion permeate all of her work. As the autobiographies chart her development as a woman, a major theme that arises is the independence, strength, and survival of African-American women. Angelou often focuses on the theme of motherhood and the relationships among African-American women. By depicting her personal history and her many roles and identities, Angelou reconstructs the image of the black woman and depicts the multiple layers of oppression, survival, and freedom.

I Know Why the Caged Bird Sings
Summary and Analysis

Maya Angelou's autobiography tells the story of the first 17 years of her life. The episodic structure of the book conveys a powerful record of her struggles and triumphs and depicts how the many painful experiences, combined with the moments of joy, shaped her into an independent, proud woman.

As a young black girl growing up in the racist South, Angelou felt insecure and inferior. She begins her story with an anecdote that captures these feelings: the young girl, Marguerite, nicknamed Maya, stands in front of her church's congregation and, feeling trapped, cannot recite her poem. She lives in a world that equates beauty with whiteness and feels displaced even among African Americans: "If growing up is painful for the Southern Black girl, being aware of her displacement is the rust on the razor that threatens the throat." Overwhelmed by feelings of inferiority and alienation, Maya runs from the church, laughing, crying, and wetting herself.

The first chapter begins with one of Angelou's earliest memories. When Maya was three and her brother, Bailey, was four, their parents divorced and sent them to live with their paternal grandmother, Annie Henderson ("Momma"), in Stamps, Arkansas. They arrive by train, wearing name tags on their wrists and a note addressed "To Whom It May Concern." This early separation greatly impacts the young Maya, contributing to feelings of abandonment and loss throughout her childhood; the scene also establishes the book's motif of a journey, in which each new place is a step toward greater self-awareness.

Maya's childhood in Stamps is a mixture of stability, love, and racist oppression. Under the care of their grandmother and Uncle Willie, the children experience unconditional love. Both Momma and Uncle Willie are devotedly religious, hardworking, and protective of the children. They are also strict and expect the children to be well-behaved. Momma owns a general store, the only store in the black section of Stamps.

At the store at a young age, Maya witnesses the cruelty of the world in the treatment of her physically disabled Uncle Willie, the "whipping boy and butt of jokes of the underemployed and underpaid." She also observes the injustices suffered by the black community, taking note of their poverty. The scenes capture the oppression of black rural life in the South during the 1930s. The Jim Crow era, which lasted from between 1877 and the 1960s, brought severe segregation laws, and the intense racism made it difficult for African Americans to own property or to earn adequate wages. The racial caste system in the South meant African Americans were viewed and treated as second-class citizens.

Most in the community pick cotton and earn very little for backbreaking work. Angelou recalls their struggle, "the fingers cut by the mean little cotton balls." Angelou's memories depict how difficult life was for African Americans in the Deep South but also reveal the closeness of the community. A feeling of hope returns each morning, only to evaporate by afternoon and the harsh reality of their difficult labor: "In cotton-picking time the late afternoons revealed the harshness of Black Southern life, which in the early morning had been softened by nature's blessing of grogginess, forgetfulness, and the soft lamplight."

Arkansas in the 1930s was an extremely segregated and racist place: "In Stamps the segregation was so complete that most Black children didn't really, absolutely know what whites looked like." As a store owner, Momma is shown slightly more respect from the white community than the average citizen, yet this respect is limited, and often she is regarded with contempt. Maya grows up under the threats of terrifying lynch mobs, in addition to the daily realities of discrimination and humiliation. One day the sheriff, a white man, stops by to warn Momma to hide Willie because a lynch mob is hunting for a black man who "messed with a white lady." Each racist incident the young girl and her family faces contributes to her expanding self-awareness.

Another incident that impacts Maya is when the "powhitetrash" girls, who live on property that her grandmother owns, show up to taunt the older woman; they mock her posture, address her by her first name, and one girl reveals her pubic hair. During all of this, Momma hums a hymn, a pillar of strength despite the racism she faces. The girls finally leave, saying, "Bye, Annie." She tells them goodbye, calling each one "Miss," a sign of respect. Bitter and humiliated that her grandmother was rendered powerless, Maya bursts into angry tears. But Momma, her face shining, tells her to wipe her face, and Maya realizes, "Whatever the contest had been out front, I knew Momma had won." Critic Dolly A. McPherson points out how this scene captures racial tensions of the South; the white girls are "practicing the rituals of white power with the full sanction of the white community and attempting to reduce the black woman to their level. On the other hand, the black woman chooses the dignified course of silent endurance" (29). Maya learns from her grandmother that maintaining one's dignity can be an effective way to respond, instead of with helpless humiliation and anger.

Despite the environment of oppression, Angelou holds many rich memories of her childhood and poetically evokes her warm feelings for the store, the central gathering place for the black community: "Until I was thirteen and left Arkansas for good, the Store was my favorite place to be." She also recalls the foods of her childhood (including her favorite, canned pineapple rings) and the books that she and her brother read so voraciously. Bailey and Maya are both extremely precocious, devouring poetry and the works of Charlotte and Emily Brontë, Mark Twain, Jane Austen, Rudyard Kipling, Edgar Allan Poe, and William Shakespeare.

Maya considers her brother "the greatest person in my world." Bailey is charismatic, loving, and protective of his sister. Much more social than Maya, Bailey displays a deep compassion for his sister, who is shy and insecure about her looks. Already at this young age, Maya equates beauty with whiteness. The prevalent racism in the community affects her sense of self and contributes to her feelings of inferiority.

In chapter 8, the Depression hits, and both the black and white communities are devastated. Through wise and honest business practices, Momma is able to save the store, while many white business owners lose everything. The family makes sacrifices but never goes hungry.

For the most part, both Maya and Bailey are happy in Stamps, but they have never understood why their parents sent them away, and they struggle with the pain of abandonment. When her mother sends Maya a white doll and a tea set for Christmas, the young girl is both angry and sad. It is easier for Maya to believe her mother is dead: "I couldn't believe that our mother would laugh and eat oranges in the sunshine without her children." Maya hides her anger and resentment, turning it into passivity.

In chapter 9, when Maya is eight and Bailey is nine, their father, Big Bailey Johnson, unexpectedly returns. Maya has no memories of her father before this, and he is like a stranger to his children. Flashy, vain, and speaking in "proper English," he tries hard to make a favorable impression. Though he acts as if he is rich, their father works as a porter at a hotel in California—even outside of the South, very few professional opportunities existed for African Americans.

The children's world turns upside-down when their father drives them to St. Louis, where their mother, Vivian Baxter, lives. She is beautiful, alluring, and glamorous: Bailey "fell instantly and forever in love"; he calls her "Mother Dear," which finally becomes "M'Deah." Both children adore her, though Maya expresses more ambivalence than Bailey. Their mother shows them love and kindness, though she is also inattentive. She lives a wild life, working in gambling parlors.

The children learn to negotiate the urban, chaotic setting of St. Louis during the height of Prohibition. Maya is introduced to new foods such as "thin-sliced ham (I thought it was a delicacy), jelly beans and peanuts mixed, lettuce on sandwich bread," and she and Bailey prove to be far more advanced than the other children in school. They also get to know their extended family. Their grandfather is from the West Indies, and their Grandmother Baxter, who has both white and black heritage, was raised by a German family. She is a commanding, strong woman who is involved with underground organized crime figures, "numbers runners, gamblers, lottery takers, and whisky salesmen," all who show her respect. She also wields power within the white community and among many of the city's politicians. Maya and Bailey also meet their two uncles, known for their meanness and for their fierce loyalty to the family. They are kind to the children, and Maya learns from them how she got her nickname; when she was a toddler, her brother called her "Mya Sister," then "My," which changed into "Maya." Her uncle assures Maya that she should not worry about being pretty, because she is smart. The advice helps the precocious girl to feel better about herself.

Maya feels like she does not have a place where she belongs and becomes used to being shuttled around throughout her life; her flexibility in accepting this helps her to deal with the world. After having the children live with their grandparents, their mother moves the children into her house, where she lives with her boyfriend, Mr. Freeman, who "moved gracefully, like a big brown bear, and seldom spoke to us." Mr. Freeman is insecure about his relationship with the children's mother, and his entire existence is based on waiting for her to come home.

Because Maya has nightmares, her mother lets her sleep with her and Mr. Freeman. One day when her mother leaves, Mr. Freeman wakes Maya and sexually abuses her. Maya, eight years old, is confused: "He held me so softly that I wished he wouldn't ever let me go." Afterward, he threatens a baffled Maya that if she tells anyone what he did, he will kill her brother. Maya feels a mix of fear and love; this is one of her first instances of "physical contact," which she mistakes for love. Freeman violates her trust and need for physical affection. After this incident, he ignores her until she sits on his lap one day, and he again molests her.

Then, when Maya is again left alone with Mr. Freeman, he rapes her: "The act of rape on an eight-year-old body is a matter of the needle giving because the camel can't." The line, an allusion to the biblical verse that a rich man getting to heaven is like a camel going through the eye of the needle, speaks of Mr. Freeman's lack of moral conduct in violating the young girl. Maya slips into unconsciousness and is sure she has died; when she wakes up, Freeman is washing her, and he again threatens that he will kill her and her brother if she says anything. He sends her to the library, but Maya experiences such intense physical pain that she goes to bed. Her mother worries she has caught the measles, but when Bailey pulls off the bed's soiled sheets, he discovers the underwear that she had hidden beneath them. Bailey promises her that whoever violated her will not actually kill him, and when she confesses it was Mr. Freeman, he "cried at the side of my bed."

Mr. Freeman goes on trial and eight-year-old Maya is questioned by the prosecutor, who tries to blame her for seducing Mr. Freeman. Frightened and confused, she lies and says that there were no incidents of prior abuse before the rape because she does not want her family to disapprove. Mr. Freeman is sentenced to one year of prison but then is temporarily released the same day. Later, a policeman shows up to tell Grandma Baxter that Mr. Freeman has been found beaten to death, most likely killed by Maya's own uncles. Traumatized, Maya believes "a man was dead because I lied" and vows to stop talking to everyone except Bailey. She becomes practically mute for the next five years, as she endures the guilt and shame of sexual abuse. Her mother's family at first accepts the silence as trauma from the rape but then becomes frustrated at what they perceive to be disrespectful behavior.

The children are sent back to Stamps in chapter 14. Bailey is heartbroken to return, but for Maya, "[t]he barrenness of Stamps was exactly what I wanted." She feels relieved to return to the order and stability. Maya has been significantly altered by the rape: She cannot remember names, colors seem faded, and she barely speaks. But her grandmother manages to break through her silence by introducing her to Mrs. Bertha Flowers, "the aristocrat of Black Stamps," who, through her affection and attention, attempts to restore a sense of normalcy to the child's life. Angelou feels indebted to her because she "threw me my first life line." Mrs. Flowers instills in Maya feelings of black pride and a love for poetry and books and also teaches her "lessons in living." Angelou recalls, "It would be safe to say that she made me proud to be Negro, just by being herself."

Back in Stamps, Maya's journey to self-awareness continues, and she begins to show resistance to the racism around her. When Mrs. Cullinan, a white woman she is working for, decides to call her Mary because Marguerite is "too long," Maya feels enraged. By renaming her, the white woman undermines Maya's identity and calls up the painful history of whites naming slaves: "Mrs. Cullinan's attempt to change Maya's name for her own convenience echoes the larger tradition of American racism that attempts to prescribe the nature and limitations of a black person's identity" (McPherson 37). Maya retaliates by purposefully dropping the woman's good china. This is Maya's first act of resistance. Though Maya is outwardly silent, she begins to display signs of a powerful inner strength.

Maya also grows more aware of both the strength and fragility of the black community. She witnesses black pride at a revival when a preacher speaks implicitly against white hypocrisy. The congregation feels renewed and inspired, but after the revival, when they must walk past a white honky-tonk party, those feelings dissipate. On the night of Joe Lewis's heavyweight championship boxing match, the entire black community crowds into the store to listen to the fight on the radio. When Lewis wins, everyone is ecstatic: "Champion of the world. A Black boy. Some Black mother's son." Joe Lewis's victory symbolizes a victory for all African Americans, a display of power and strength over the oppressor.

By becoming a part of the community, Maya develops a stronger sense of black pride and identity. The community members in Stamps help one another and come together both in times of celebration and of mourning. At the summer picnic fish fry, for example, everyone in the community shows up in an expression of solidarity. It is there that Maya makes her first friend, Louise Kendricks. The girls hold hands and spin in circles, looking at the sky. Maya rediscovers the girlhood and innocence that Mr. Freeman stole from her: "girls have to giggle, and after being a woman for three years I was about to become a girl." She tries to push the rape out of her mind and "had generally come to believe that the nightmare with its attendant guilt and fear hadn't really happened to me." She experiences delight when one of her classmates gets a crush on her, restoring some of her self-worth and the innocence that Mr. Freeman took from her. Meanwhile, Bailey spends more time away from Maya as he comes of age. He loses his virginity to Joyce, who runs off with a railroad porter and breaks his heart.

In chapter 23, the entire community is brewing with excitement about graduation. However, at Maya's eighth-grade ceremony, the white speaker, Donleavy, insults and devastates the community by insinuating that the only future for African-American students is to become athletes or servants: "The white kids were to have a chance to become Galileos and Madame Curies and Edisons, and Gauguins, and our boys (the girls weren't even in on it) would try to be Jessie Owenses and Joe Louises." Angelou explains how painful this is for the black audience, as the speaker evokes feelings of bitterness and defeat. After the speaker leaves, however, the eighth-grade valedictorian, Henry Reed, leads the audience in the "Negro National Anthem," a song based on a poem written by James Weldon Johnson, restoring their confidence. In this moment, Maya realizes, "I was no longer simply a member of the proud graduating class of 1940; I was a proud member of the wonderful, beautiful Negro race."

Maya experiences firsthand the cruelty of racism when she is suffering from a painful toothache and the white dentist in town refuses to treat her. Her grandmother asks for this favor, reminding him that she lent him money during the Depression, but he tells her, "I'd rather stick my hand in a dog's mouth than in a nigger's." Quietly, Momma follows him into the office, while Maya waits outside and fantasizes about Momma taking revenge and overpowering him. She discovers later that Momma told the dentist that he owed her interest and then used the 10 dollars to take Maya on the train to see the black dentist in Texarkana. Though Maya prefers her fantasy, for her grandmother to stand up to the white man was a powerful statement; Momma and Uncle Willie laugh about it, feeling that she scored a victory. The interest she charged him is symbolic: She makes him pay for his hatred and disrespect.

The intense racism and violence of the South prove to be inescapable. One day Bailey sees white men fish the rotting corpse of a black man out of the river.

The men make jokes and express their satisfaction. Bailey is traumatized and utterly confused by this kind of hatred. He begins posing questions that are dangerous for a black boy in the 1930s South to ask. Momma fears for the children's well-being, and she saves money to take the children to California to be with their mother.

They take a train to Los Angeles, where their father lives, and stay there for about six months. After Momma returns to Arkansas, the children move to Oakland to live with their mother and Grandmother Baxter. Their mother is a trained surgical nurse but earns a living by playing pinochle or running poker games. She is fearless, fun, and exciting. One night she wakes them at 2:30 a.m. to surprise them with biscuits and chocolate milk. After the start of World War II, their mother marries Daddy Clidell, and they move with the children to the Fillmore district of San Francisco, a city where Maya feels truly at home. The various foods she is introduced to there symbolize how Maya's world has diversified. Now she eats Chinese food, Italian pizza, Hungarian goulash, and Irish stew: "Through food we learned that there were other people in the world."

San Francisco, in a state of transition during World War II, is a much different place from the South, and it is there that Maya thrives. The schools are not segregated, and there are more opportunities for African Americans, especially as more factory jobs open up. However, Maya notices the displacement of the Japanese, who were forced into internment camps during the war, and how nobody in the African-American community speaks out about this injustice. From an early age, Maya has noticed and felt pained by any kind of injustice.

In San Francisco, Maya gains a sense of empowerment. She watches how Daddy Clidell and his friends make money off white men. The first positive father figure in her life, Daddy Clidell teaches Maya how to play poker, blackjack, and other card games. Maya attends George Washington High School, where she is one of three black students. She is awarded a scholarship to the California Labor School, where she takes drama and dance classes.

One summer, Maya stays with her father and his girlfriend, Dolores, in Los Angeles. Maya and Dolores do not get along, and the tension culminates after her father, usually indifferent to her, takes Maya on a "shopping trip" across the border to Mexico. Her father goes to a bar where the locals know him. He drinks, sings, dances, and then goes off with a woman. By the end of the day, he is too drunk to drive and passes out. Maya, no longer a passive little girl, jumps to action. Although she has never driven before, she drives down the mountain, feeling fearless. This significant scene portrays the way Maya has changed and grown: She now has the power to assert control over her life. She has turned into a defiant, strong, young woman who feels confident in herself. At the border, she hits another car, but her father wakes, and, in his charming manner, diffuses any anger by sharing his liquor.

Her father, however, cannot diffuse Dolores's anger. She calls Maya's mother a whore, and Maya reacts by slapping her. Dolores then cuts her, and, too embarrassed to take her to the hospital, her father enlists a friend to fix the wound. This action reveals her father's selfishness and his lack of regard for his children. He then takes Maya to stay at another friend's, but Maya, asserting her independence, decides to leave. She wanders the streets until she finds a car in a junkyard, where she spends the night. At the junkyard, she meets other homeless young people, and "after a month my thinking processes had so changed that I was hardly recognizable to myself. The unquestioning acceptance by my peers had dislodged the familiar insecurity." Maya enters a new phase of her life, marked by resourcefulness, an independent spirit, and fearlessness. She meets young people from different races and backgrounds and can be herself with them: "The lack of criticism evidenced by our ad hoc community influenced me, and set a tone of tolerance for my life."

She returns to her mother, feeling assured and confident: "I had reasoned that I had given up some youth for knowledge, but my gain was more valuable than the loss." Bailey is also growing up, now running with "a group of slick street boys." After he gets into an argument with his beloved mother, he moves out. They reconcile but decide it is best for him to live on his own. Bailey eventually joins the merchant marines.

Maya decides to get a job as a streetcar conductor, but her initial attempt is unsuccessful when she is informed that they do not hire African Americans. Maya does not let this stop her: For three weeks, she shows up to the city office and appeals to various organizations for support. Finally, her determination pays off, and she becomes "the first Negro on the San Francisco streetcars." The position exposes and gives her access to a larger world, as she "clanged and cleared my way down Market Street." By defying racist hiring policies and becoming the first black streetcar conductor, at age 15, she has found independence and freedom and continues on her journey to adulthood.

Maya is developing into a strong, independent woman, yet she also feels awkward facing puberty and the changes of adolescence. She is tall, has a low voice, and feels somewhat awkward. After she reads *The Well of Loneliness*, Maya fears that she is a lesbian (which she thinks is a hermaphrodite) and, at 16, in an attempt to assert her sexuality, has sex with a teenaged boy she knows only vaguely. Three weeks later, she discovers she is pregnant. She hides the pregnancy for eight months before telling her mother and stepfather, who are both supportive of her.

When the baby is born, Maya is afraid of touching him because he is so small. But her mother puts the baby next to her in the bed, and when Maya wakes up later that night, she is protectively holding him. Maya accepts her role as a mother and begins the transition to adulthood. By ending with a birth, the book concludes on a hopeful note, contrasting with the opening scene. Now Maya has accepted, with love and pride, her identity as a woman, an African American, and a mother.

Major Themes

Angelou wrote *I Know Why the Caged Bird Sings* at the end of the civil rights movement; the impetus for the book was the assassination of her friend Martin Luther King Jr. The title of *I Know Why the Caged Bird Sings* comes from the poem "Sympathy" by Paul Laurence Dunbar, an African-American poet of the late nineteenth and early twentieth centuries. The title is a metaphor for the book: Even in the imprisonment of racism that Maya experiences, she still finds her voice and, like the bird, makes herself heard even in the midst of struggle.

The autobiography concerns Angelou's traumatic experiences of childhood rape and growing up in the racist climate of the South and portrays how she overcame obstacles and evolved into a strong, independent woman. One of the book's central themes is the injustice of racism and the history of African-American resilience and resistance to this oppression. As a young girl, she feels only hopeless rage, with subtle forms of resistance, but, by the end, she is engaged in active protest. She goes from feeling like a victim to someone who feels pride and confidence. Angelou also explores the isolation and loneliness she felt in her life and how she coped as a survivor of sexual abuse. The power and legacy of strong independent African-American women is a major theme, as are community, motherhood, and the power of language.

The Legacy of Strong African-American Women

It shocks Angelou when people seem surprised to encounter strong black women. For black women to survive in a racist, sexist society, she explains, they must be strong: "The fact that the adult American Negro female emerges as a formidable character is often met with amazement, distance, and even belligerence. It is seldom accepted as an inevitable outcome of the struggle won by survivors and deserves respect if not enthusiastic acceptance."

Angelou begins the autobiography by highlighting her insecurity, how she felt she could never match up to the pretty white girls and only wants to wake from this "black dream." The scene captures a young black girl's disillusionment with American society, which defined beauty in terms of white physical appearance. Yet by the end of the autobiography, Maya feels proud to be a black woman and is herself a role model, like the women in her family. Maya learns early on that black women have many obstacles they must face and surmount, and if they are to survive, they must develop forms of resistance and protest. Almost all of the women in Maya's life contribute to her growth, independence, and sense of strength in varying ways.

Grandmother Henderson serves as Maya's main role model, moral guide, and mother figure throughout her childhood. Momma instills in Maya early feelings of black pride, and, though at times Maya feels that her grandmother is acting too submissively, Momma, "a realist," knows how to choose her battles and how to survive in the racist South. For example, Momma and Willie bravely hide a black man fleeing a lynch mob, and later "Mrs. Henderson" is issued a subpoena by the judge. When the white court realizes this "Mrs." refers to a black woman, the officials think it is a joke, because in their racist view, "Mrs." is only used to refer to white women. However, the African-American community remembers and regards her with great respect—the title an indication of her stature and dignity. When Maya leaves with her father, she is scared and resistant to parting from her grandmother. Though Momma is not an affectionate woman, "a deep-brooding love hung over everything she touched." After Maya is raped, she longs for the stability of the store and Momma, and it is her grandmother who helps young Maya recover her voice. She also learns resourcefulness from Momma, who lives for six months in Los Angeles, adjusting to the strange environment and making "the same kinds of friends she had always had."

Maya's Grandmother Baxter, though much different from the religious Momma, is also a model of strength. She chooses not to pass as white and wields power with the underground crime scene and the white community. Both Grandmother Baxter and Henderson are businesswomen, each in her own way. Although Maya's mother is not a part of her life until Maya enters adolescence, her mother also proves to be a role model. Her beauty, confidence, and fiery attitude influence Maya and compel her to stand up for what she believes in and to take the less-traveled path. Though Maya's mother is not as stable a presence as her grandmother, her mother stands by Maya when she becomes pregnant. Her mother promises Maya that she will not hurt her daughter's child but naturally wants to protect him, passing on to her a mother's wisdom. Motherhood links the various women characters, and, in the end, Maya is initiated into this legacy of strong mother figures.

The Power of Words

Maya develops a love for reading early in life, and books often relieve her from feelings of loneliness and isolation. She reveals: "I met and fell in love with William Shakespeare. He was my first white love." She feels guilty about his whiteness but feels moved by his language. As young children, she and Bailey read voraciously, and books connect her to the warmth and lovingness of the store and family life. Maya also turns to books as her brother grows more independent and, in St. Louis, spends much of her time at the library. Books are both an escape and a comfort.

After Maya is raped and disappears into silence, Mrs. Flowers awakens her by reading to her and introducing her to poetry. When Mrs. Flowers reads aloud to her from A Tale of Two Cities, which the young girl had already read, Maya feels like she is hearing an entirely different book: "I heard poetry for the first time in my life." She chooses to be mute because she fears the destructive power of words, but Mrs. Flowers teaches her about the positive aspects of language, empowering her to speak again. Thus, poetry helps her regain her voice, and this rediscovery brings Maya back to life.

The power of words and literature also bring her closer to her community. At her graduation, she listens closely to the words of James Weldon Johnson and witnesses the way the "Black National Anthem" unites the black community, evoking pride and hope. Not only does the poem bind Maya more intensely to the community around her, but it marks the first time she, having previously read only white writers, hears African-American poetry. She is inspired and moved and will go on to contribute her own words and poetic sensibilities to a wider world she grows to embrace and inhabit.

TONI MORRISON

Biography

Toni Morrison (born Chloe Anthony Wofford) was born on February 18, 1931, to George and Ramah Willis Wofford in Lorain, Ohio, the second of four children in a working-class family. An avid reader as a child, Morrison entered Howard University in 1949, where she majored in English with a minor in classics. She then went on to continue her education at Cornell University, where she wrote her thesis on William Faulkner and Virginia Woolf. Morrison received her M.A. in 1955, taught English at Texas Southern University in Houston, and returned to Washington, D.C., to accept an English faculty position at Howard University. In 1958, she married Harold Morrison, a Jamaican architect, and they had two children. The couple divorced in 1964.

In 1965, Morrison moved to Syracuse, New York, to become a textbook editor of a subsidiary of Random House. Two years later, she transferred to New York City and was promoted to senior editor, where she specialized in publishing and editing black writers, including Angela Davis, Toni Cade Bambara, and Gayle Jones. During this time, she also taught part time at two separate branches of the State University of New York. Morrison remained at Random House until 1984, when she was appointed to the Albert Schweitzer Chair of the Humanities at the State University of New York at Albany.

Morrison began writing fiction as part of an informal group of writers when she was teaching at Howard University. For one meeting, she showed up with a story about a black girl who longed to have blue eyes. This story would eventually evolve into her first novel, *The Bluest Eye* (1970), which she wrote while raising her two children. In 1973, Morrison's novel *Sula* was nominated for the National Book Award. Her third novel, *Song of Solomon* (1977), brought her national attention when it was selected for the Book-of-the-Month Club, the first novel by a black writer to be chosen since Richard Wright's *Native Son* in 1940. *Song of Solomon* also won the National Book Critics Circle Award and the American Academy and Institute of Arts and Letters Award. She followed this success with the publication of *Tar Baby* (1981).

Morrison's popularity and critical acclaim escalated with the publication of *Beloved* in 1988. When the novel failed to win the National Book Award as well as the National Book Critics Circle Award, a number of writers protested the omission. Shortly after, it was awarded the Pulitzer Prize. *Beloved* was adapted into the popular 1998 film starring Oprah Winfrey and Danny Glover. Morrison published *Jazz* in 1992, and in 1993, she was awarded the Nobel Prize in Literature. Her other novels include *Paradise* (1998), *Love* (2003), and *A Mercy* (2008). From 1989 until her retirement in 2006, Morrison held the Robert F. Goheen Chair in the Humanities at Princeton University.

Morrison's writing is both difficult and accessible: She is known for her densely lyrical narratives and for her epic storytelling. Influences include Faulkner's modernist lyricism and Gabriel García Márquez's magical realism. Morrison often writes about magical events and mythical characters, while grounding narratives in an often brutal reality. Her novels feature shifting points of view, often blurring past and present. Memory, community, gender, and identity are major themes explored in her novels. Morrison examines the history of racism and slavery in the United States, depicting the injustice and inhumanity that prevailed, while at the same time revealing the power of love, faith, and redemption. Morrison is one of the nation's most widely read and highly regarded living authors; her novels explore the rich tapestry of the African-American experience, the lives of women, and the flaws and beauty of the human condition.

The Bluest Eye
Summary and Analysis

The Bluest Eye, set in Lorain, Ohio, at the end of the Great Depression, is the tragic story of Pecola Breedlove, an 11-year-old girl who prays for blue eyes because she thinks they will bring beauty and love to her life. Morrison shifts points of view, allowing different aspects of Pecola's story to emerge. The principal narrator is Claudia MacTeer, who tells the story as an adult looking back at portions of her childhood years; the other narrator, who is omniscient, describes the other characters in the community.

The novel is divided by the seasons, each representing another stage of loss in the girls' innocence. Chapter titles, which are phrases taken from a Dick and Jane reading primer, contrast the lifestyle of the primer's white upper-middle-class family with the difficult, often brutal world of the Breedloves. The novel begins with a page from the primer, but the sentences and words run together in gibberish, representing Pecola's doomed dream of entering this illusive, idealized world.

Pecola's story begins in "Autumn" in 1940. Claudia, nine years old, is independent and strong-willed and close to her sister, Frieda, who is older by one year. Struggling to make ends meet, their parents have just taken in a boarder, Henry Washington. Their mother, who sings the blues while she works, is strict, but both she and Mr. MacTeer provide the girls with love and stability. The MacTeers temporarily take in Pecola because her father has tried to burn down the family house. Claudia and Frieda feel sorry for Pecola—a sensitive, fragile, and lonely child.

The Bluest Eye, a coming-of-age story, reveals how, over time and in different ways, the girls' childhood innocence is lost. One of their first experiences with adulthood occurs when Pecola unexpectedly begins to menstruate. This scene reveals how the girls have been conditioned to fear sexuality and its "nasty" implications. Though Pecola displays signs of a physical maturation and transformation, she remains mentally and emotionally a child. She is drawn, for example, to the Shirley Temple mug, drinking three quarts of milk in one day in order to continue admiring it.

The characters reference popular films and white cultural icons, and the little girls receive white dolls for Christmas. Claudia, however, resents the propaganda that whiteness is superior and "destroy[s] those baby dolls." She is indignant that her parents never ask her what she wants for Christmas but assume that the white dolls will please her. Having no connection to the dolls, she dismembers them "to find the beauty." She wants to know why white girls are fawned over. As she transfers her anger at the dolls to little white girls, she is shamefully aware of her own feelings of hatred and her capacity for violence.

The omniscient narrator describes Pecola's family, the Breedloves. The members of this family internalize the racist culture they live in. Their home is a cramped, squalid storefront, and they live there "because they were poor and black, and they stayed there because they believed they were ugly." Pecola's father, Cholly, is a drunk, and her parents fight violently. Pecola's brother, Sammy, frequently runs away, but Pecola's only escape is to pray for blue eyes. In her childish naiveté, she believes beauty merits love, and she wants to be as loved as the blond, blue-eyed children she sees in her community and portrayed in popular entertainment. Pecola's belief that others feel nothing but distaste toward her is confirmed when the white shopkeeper refuses to touch her hand. Every interaction in the novel seems to confirm the view that whiteness is beautiful and that blackness, its opposite, is not. As a result, Pecola, who has dark skin, feels alone and unwanted. The only adults who show Pecola any kindness are the prostitutes who live above the store: Miss Marie (who is often referred to as the Maginot Line), China, and Poland. The women, ostracized by the community, are good natured and affectionate. Their kindness toward Pecola contrasts with the behaviors of self-righteous, respectable women such as Geraldine.

In the novel's next section, "Winter," Claudia recalls when a group of black boys surrounded Pecola, calling her ugly and black, an expression and projection of their own self-hatred. The sisters stand up to them, but the boys only stop because the new girl at school, Maureen Peal, is with them. Maureen Peal is a light-skinned girl, with braids like "two lynch ropes," an image that symbolizes the violence of a society that places values on skin color. Loved by the teachers and children, Maureen reinforces the connection between race and class—lighter skinned, she is also wealthier. After buying Pecola ice cream and acting as her friend, Maureen is only interested in making fun of Pecola's father and referring to his naked body. When Claudia and Frieda start lashing back at Maureen's verbal attack, she yells, "I am cute! And you ugly. Black and ugly!" Again and again, the message that black is ugly is hammered into the children.

The narrator then goes on to describe Geraldine, a middle-class black woman who is ashamed of her blackness. She believes in cleanliness and purity and expresses affection for nothing beyond her blue-eyed cat. As a result, her emotionally neglected son, Junior, unleashes his anger by torturing the cat and harassing other children. When Pecola passes through the playground, he cajoles her to come inside his house. The orderly, clean house contrasts with the squalor of the Breedlove home, yet there is no love or happiness in Geraldine's house either. Junior hurls his mother's cat at Pecola's face and then swings the cat by the tail before throwing it against the wall, killing it. He blames Pecola for the cat's death, and Geraldine, viewing Pecola as the embodiment of the blackness she has been trying to deny, calls her "a nasty little black bitch."

Claudia's narrative returns in "Spring," generally a time of renewal, but in the novel, it is a time of lost innocence. One of the underlying critiques Morrison expresses in the novel concerns the ways a sexist society renders women and girls powerless. When Mr. Henry touches Frieda's breasts, he corrupts her innocence. Claudia and Frieda's father kicks him out of their house, and in one of the few comic points in the novel, the girls then worry that Frieda will now become fat like Maginot Line.

Looking for Pecola, the MacTeer sisters go to the house of the white family where Pecola's mother works. The large, clean house replicates the one portrayed in the Dick and Jane reader. While they wait in the kitchen, a little white girl enters and is immediately afraid. She calls for Pecola's mother, referring to her as "Polly." This shortened nickname reveals that she is not expected to show respect for an African-American adult and also suggests the girl shares an intimacy with Pecola's mother that Pecola, who calls her mother "Mrs. Breedlove," is not allowed. When Pecola accidentally knocks over the berry cobbler, Mrs. Breedlove knocks her down then comforts the "little girl in pink," promising to get the stain out of her dress. Like Geraldine, Mrs. Breedlove associates cleanliness and beauty with whiteness. When the white girl asks who the black girls are, Mrs. Breedlove does not answer, renouncing her own daughter.

The omniscient narrator provides background on Pecola's parents. Pauline Breedlove, from Kentucky, grew up with a lame foot and felt isolated and physically unattractive. She eventually met Cholly, but after they moved north, her loneliness deepened, prompting her to escape her sadness by going to the movies and imitating white movie stars. In her present life, considering herself a martyr, she encourages Cholly's violence and finds her self-worth in taking care of the white family: "Pauline kept this order, this beauty, for herself, a private world, and never introduced it into her storefront, or to her children."

Abandoned as an infant, Cholly Breedlove was rescued by his aunt, whom he lived with until she died. His most traumatizing experience occurs at her funeral, where, against an idyllic setting, he happily goes off with Darlene. While the two become physically intimate, two white hunters come upon them and command Cholly to "finish." Humiliated and powerless, Cholly takes out his hatred on Darlene instead of the men: "They were big, white, armed men. He was small, black, helpless." He runs away to find his father, who rebukes him, making Cholly into even more of a dangerous, unstable person. The reader sympathizes with Cholly because he has suffered, but then Morrison shows him coming home drunk. Seeing his daughter at the sink washing dishes, he rapes her, and Morrison shows the attack, an expression of "hatred mixed with tenderness," through Cholly's eyes. Afterward, he covers Pecola with a blanket and leaves her passed out on the kitchen floor.

The omniscient narrator next describes Soaphead Church, the "cinnamon-eyed West Indian with lightly browned skin" brought up to deny his own blackness. He poses as "Reader, Adviser, and Interpreter of Dreams," and when Pecola comes to him asking for blue eyes, he feels touched: "Here was an ugly little girl asking for beauty." But he takes advantage of her, tricking her into poisoning a neighborhood dog he dislikes. He writes a rambling, egotistical letter to God, in which he expresses his outrage at the racism of the world but does not acknowledge his own wrongdoing. A hypocrite, Soaphead perpetuates society's brutality by molesting little girls.

In the novel's next section, "Summer," Claudia and Frieda order packets of seeds, hoping to sell them so that they can buy a bicycle. From the gossiping adults, they learn about Pecola's rape and pregnancy, this "secret, terrible, awful story." The neighborhood gossips are disgusted by Cholly's actions but also blame Pecola. The women doubt the baby will live, because it will be too "ugly." The sisters feel shame, then sorrow. They pray for the baby to live, and Claudia tells herself that the baby is beautiful inside the womb, much more beautiful than the white dolls. The sisters plant the seeds, believing that if the plants grow, then Pecola's baby will also survive.

Pecola is then seen arguing with an imaginary friend. She has been beaten nearly to death by her mother and taken out of school, and Cholly, after raping her a second time, has run away and will later die in a workhouse. The flowers do not bloom, and the baby dies. "The damage done was total," and Pecola succumbs to mental illness. Only with a clouded mind can she convince herself that now she is beautiful with blue eyes. Instead of allowing her to see clearly, these eyes are a form of blindness. Her transformation into a figure of tragedy is complete, as she avoids the consequence of her knowledge and the horrible abuse she has suffered; she spends her days invisible to the world, walking up and down the streets, searching through garbage.

In the final passage, the viewpoint shifts back to Claudia. She considers the long-lasting damage done to Pecola, acknowledging the community's participation; Pecola served as a scapegoat, a way for the community to escape its own self-hatred: "We were so beautiful when we stood astride her ugliness." Claudia must now bear the full weight of her knowledge about the world. Though the ending is bleak, there is hope that words and stories can heal this broken community.

Major Themes

Toni Morrison wrote *The Bluest Eye* during the Black Arts movement of the 1960s. Its members promoted a reclaiming and celebration of African-American beauty, and one of the movement's rallying cries became "Black Is Beautiful." By telling the story of one little girl's desire for love, Morrison reveals the broken dreams and self-hatred of an entire African-American community. The novel critiques racism and sexism, as Morrison addresses incest, racial segregation, class issues, and questions of identity. Principal themes about race, gender, and childhood innocence are evoked throughout the narrative.

White Standards of Beauty

Whiteness as the measure of beauty had become so entrenched in American society that many African Americans were negatively influenced by these standards of physical attractiveness based on skin color, which they could never achieve. The community in the novel values light skin over dark skin, as symbolized by the "dream child" Maureen Peal. Morrison portrays the self-hatred that had become deeply rooted in many of the community's members and reveals the way African-American women have been taught to hate or devalue their own bodies or physical attributes. The characters in the novel often take this hatred out on their children. Geraldine, ashamed of her blackness, calls Pecola a "nasty little black bitch," and Pecola's mother exhibits more love for the white daughter of her employer than for her own children.

Pecola has internalized that she is "black and ugly" and believes that if she had blue eyes, she would be beautiful and her life would be somehow different and better: "Each night, without fail, she prayed for blue eyes." When eating Mary Jane candies, she hopes to digest whiteness and become like the little white girl on the wrapper: "To eat the candy is somehow to eat the eyes, eat Mary Jane. Love Mary Jane. Be Mary Jane." She tragically believes that if she possesses blue eyes, the cruelty in her life will be replaced by love. This hopeless desire ultimately leads to tragedy and mental illness.

Messages suggesting that whiteness is superior or the societal ideal are everywhere in the United States, especially so at the time in which the novel is set.

This representation and exposure included movies and pop culture, as Morrison shows with the cultural icon Shirley Temple and the white dolls Claudia grows to resent: "Adults, older girls, shops, magazines, newspapers, window signs—all the world had agreed that a blue-eyed, yellow-haired, pink-skinned doll was what every girl child treasured." But Claudia resists the premise of white superiority; she creates her own story about the beauty of blackness and prays for Pecola's baby to live: "I felt a need for someone to want the black baby to live—just to counteract the universal love of white baby dolls, Shirley Temples, and Maureen Peals."

Sexual Violence and the Loss of Innocence

The MacTeer sisters and Pecola are innocent at the beginning of the novel, but by the end, they are saddled with a new awareness of the powerlessness of women in a male-dominated society. The prevalence of sexual violence threatens and damages their individual girlhoods; their transition into sexual maturity is often violent and abusive. Pecola is a child raped by her father. Frieda is fondled by Henry Washington. Soaphead Church also preys on little girls. These experiences are hurtful and shameful, depicting a sexual coming of age that is marked with peril or abuse. Though most of the sexual violence focuses on girls, Cholly also experiences a violent sexual act as a young man and, years later, reenacts this humiliation to an even more brutal degree when he rapes his daughter.

The girls have no role models or positive examples of proper romantic and sexual conduct. Instead, they live with the assumption that women's bodies are available for abuse. When Pecola first menstruates, the sudden development causes fear, confusion, and accusations of "nastiness." The prostitutes in town are treated as outsiders, which the girls quickly learn. When Maginot Line invites them in for a soda, Frieda tells her they cannot because "My mama said you ruined." Furthermore, respectable women, such as Geraldine, view sexuality as dirty or shameful. Thus, the girls are influenced to believe that sexuality, and perhaps even the state of womanhood itself, is something immoral and "nasty." The only positive portrayal of sex in the novel occurs before the white men show up, when the intimacy Cholly and Darleen experience is joyous and consensual. The novel suggests that coming of age should not be frightening or abusive but a natural and positive process of self-realization and self-fulfillment. Such an ideal situation, however, is not possible in a sexist environment that oppresses girls and women.

Beloved
Summary and Analysis

Beloved takes place primarily in Cincinnati in 1873, eight years after the end of the Civil War, and opens with the past literally haunting the present. The protagonist, Sethe, and her 18-year-old daughter, Denver, live in a "spiteful" house that is haunted by Sethe's infant daughter, furious "at having its throat cut." Sethe's two sons have already run off.

As the novel begins, Paul D, whom Sethe has not seen since they were both slaves 18 years before, shows up. His arrival causes Sethe to remember a past she has tried to forget. The narrative unfolds in two different times and settings: the present day in Cincinnati, and the past in Kentucky, which is revealed through fragmented flashbacks. These flashbacks eventually add up to a complete narrative that details the trauma that Sethe, Paul D, and the other slaves suffered.

Sethe and Paul D were both slaves at the ironically named Sweet Home, a Kentucky plantation that was owned by a seemingly benevolent couple, Mr. and Mrs. Garner, and their slaves: Baby Suggs, her son Halle, Paul A, Paul D, Paul F, and Sixo. After Halle buys his mother's freedom, the Garners replace Baby Suggs with 13-year-old Sethe. When Mr. Garner dies, the cruel, brutal overseer schoolteacher takes over, and the relative stability of Sweet Home devolves into a nightmare of humiliation, beatings, and murders.

For Sethe, the worst assault is when the schoolteacher ordered his nephews to steal the milk from her breasts. The harrowing memory evokes the novel's motifs of motherhood. For Sethe, this assault and physical violation is worse than the beating that followed—the nephews whip her, leaving a "tree" of scars. The "tree" is one of many physical reminders of the horror of slavery, and when Paul D touches it, he "learned that way her sorrow, the roots of it." Sethe always assumed that Halle abandoned her. By comparing memories with Paul D, she realizes that Halle witnessed the assault, which explains why the last time Paul D saw Halle he was angry, sitting by the churn with "butter all over his face." Paul D could not help his friend because he was chained with a bit in his mouth, an image of slavery that triggers his own anger and pain.

After she is beaten by the schoolteacher's nephews, Sethe runs off, nine months pregnant. She reaches the Ohio River and is rescued by a white girl, Amy Denver, a 16-year-old indentured servant who delivers her baby. The baby, named Denver, is born in a boat with the Ohio River's water washing over her, representing the first generation of freedom. Sethe's escape from Sweet Home and the infant she has just given birth to reveal her resistance to slavery's attempt to control black motherhood. Stamp Paid, a conductor for the Underground Railroad—a system of safe houses that hid and supported slaves until they could reach free states or Canada—ferries Sethe across the Ohio River. Sethe then meets Baby Suggs and is reunited with her children. She experiences the freedom of "unslaved life." She becomes a part of the community, in which Baby Suggs is the "unchurched preacher." Baby Suggs leads her followers to a clearing in the forest, a sanctuary for spiritual healing, where she encourages her congregation to love themselves and their children, offering them "her great big heart."

Paul D's terrifying time at Sweet Home and his escape are also presented in a series of flashbacks. Although he copes by locking his emotions away in the "tobacco tin," his violent, hurtful memories of both Sweet Home and the time he spent on the chain gang in Georgia painfully reemerge. As a prisoner, Paul D was locked in a small cage, beaten, and sexually assaulted by the white prison guards. The shackled men, bound by the chain looped through their ankle cuffs, relied on the power of working together to escape while chained together. Broken and psychologically destroyed, Paul D struggles to regain his manhood.

The narrative, returning to the present day, then presents Denver, Paul D, and Sethe, returning from the carnival. They come upon an exhausted, well-dressed woman sitting outside the house who calls herself Beloved. Sethe immediately has to relieve herself, releasing an uncontrollable stream of urine that alludes to her water breaking and symbolizes the birth and now rebirth of her deceased daughter. Images of infancy surround Beloved: Her neck seems unable to support her head, her skin is soft and unlined, and she drinks as greedily as a nursing infant.

Beloved hovers around Sethe, who tells her stories in order "to feed her." When Beloved asks about Sethe's own mother, Sethe reports that she hardly knew her. Her mother, a field slave, had been raped by the white crew of the slave ship transporting her to North America. She "threw away" the babies that resulted but kept Sethe—the only one who was the child of a black man whom she loved. Beloved knows intimate details about Sethe but reveals nothing about herself. When Paul D asks her where she came from, she simply says she has come a "long, long, long, long way. Nobody bring me. Nobody help me." When Denver asks, "What's it like over there, where you were born?" Beloved describes a "hot" place: "A lot of people is down there. Some is dead." Beloved's answer could suggest the womb or a grave. For Denver, the answer confirms her belief that Beloved is her dead sister, returned in the flesh.

Lonely and isolated, Denver is happy to have a friend and confidante. Denver was born free but is enslaved by her mother's haunted memories. When Denver was young, she took lessons from a teacher named Lady Jones, but her formal education stopped after a fellow classmate asked her, "Didn't your mother get locked away for murder? Wasn't you in there with her when she went?" After this confrontation, Denver goes deaf for two years.

Fearful of hearing more about her mother, she "walked in a silence too solid for penetration." Beloved has a different effect on each of the three principal characters. She goes through several incarnations or forms: an infant, a sexual woman, a daughter, and a sister. After Paul D moves out into the shed, Beloved shows up at his door and seduces him, directing him to open his heart.

The tension between the past and present builds until the end of part 1, when the rest of Sethe's story is revealed. Twenty-eight days after Sethe's reunion with her children, schoolteacher returns to take Sethe and her children back to their life of slavery, an action that was legal under the Fugitive Slave Act of 1850. Sethe recognized schoolteacher's hat as the four horsemen approached, an allusion to the four horsemen of the apocalypse in the Bible's book of Revelation.

Terrified, Sethe ran through the yard "snatching up her children like a hawk on the wing." She fled with them to the woodshed and tried to kill them with a hand saw. Only the third child, her older daughter, dies. Sethe later arranges for the baby's headstone to be carved with the word "Beloved." Stamp Paid tells the story to Paul D and shows him the newspaper clipping, but Paul D, who cannot read, argues that the picture is not Sethe.

Sethe, however, convinces him that the story is true. For the first time, she tries to express her own repressed memory of the day when she successfully "stopped" schoolteacher from taking her children. "Your love is too thick," Paul D accuses. He says, "You got two feet, Sethe, not four," a remark that is particularly cutting because it causes Sethe to recall schoolteacher instructing his nephews to make a list of her "animal" characteristics.

Part 2 builds on Sethe's present relationship with Beloved. She accepts Beloved as the reincarnation of her murdered daughter and hopes that now she will no longer have to remember the painful incidents of her past. However, for the rest of the novel, Sethe tries relentlessly to explain to Beloved why she killed her. Denver recalls that on the day schoolteacher arrived to take Sethe and her children back to Kentucky, "I swallowed her blood right along with my mother's milk," taking on her mother's guilt and trauma. Though she may have saved her children from slavery, Sethe also lost them. Denver knows that her brothers left because their mother had attempted to kill them.

Beloved's narrative, constructed in choppy sentences and without punctuation, hints at her existence among the dead yet also strongly suggests that she was a part of the Middle Passage, the route slave ships took with their human cargo from Africa to North America. Images and phrases such as the "circle around her neck," and "storms rock us," suggest that she is describing being aboard a ship. She remembers her mother jumping into the water, abandoning her. Other phrases—"he hurts where I sleep," and "there is a house"—suggest Beloved could be a real person who has lived a secluded life in the shadows of slavery. Beloved represents the ghost of Sethe's infant daughter, but she also represents the ghost of slavery.

After Sethe's confession, Paul D distances himself from her and the community. Stamp Paid apologizes for showing him the newspaper clipping and shares with Paul D a story from his own past. When he was a slave, his master's son took Stamp's wife as a concubine, repeatedly raping her, and he could do nothing to stop this horror. Part 2 concludes with Paul D's question for himself and for his nation, "Tell me this one thing. How much is a nigger supposed to take? Tell me. How much?"

In part 3, Sethe stops going to work in order to spend all of her time with Beloved, who has become a raging tyrant. Denver realizes she must protect her mother. The house is empty of food and Denver, though afraid, makes the decision "to step off the edge of the world." She approaches Lady Jones and tells her that her mother is sick. The women in the community have isolated Sethe for 18 years, but now they leave food on the tree stump at the edge of the yard.

Denver transforms from a sheltered girl to the hero of the novel. She sets out to look for work, approaching the abolitionist couple, the Bodwins. When she tells their servant, Janey Wagon, about Beloved, Janey assumes Beloved is a demon, and she spreads the news to the other women. Ella, who had worked for the Underground Railroad, organizes a rescue. She considers the ghost of the baby "an invasion" of the dead onto the living or of the past into the present.

While Denver waits on the front porch for Mr. Bodwin to pick her up for her first day of work, the women arrive with charms and religious objects. They pray and sing, and the strength of the communal voices calls Sethe and Beloved to the doorway. When Sethe hears the voices of the women, it was "as though the Clearing had come to her." The image of the clearing, with its associations of spiritual freedom and rebirth, emphasizes the healing power of the women and signifies a new beginning.

The women act as a force against what they consider to be evil, the "devil child," yet the image that emerges of Beloved standing there naked and pregnant, "thunderback and glistening," also evokes the image of a beautiful African mother. When Mr. Bodwin arrives, Sethe mistakes him for schoolteacher. Beloved runs away, and Denver stops her mother from attacking Bodwin, thus stopping the cycle of the past overpowering the present.

Beloved is gone, and Paul D finds Sethe in Baby Suggs's bed, planning to die. Sethe calls Beloved her "best thing," and Paul disagrees: "You your best thing, Sethe. You are." Sethe's last question, "Me? Me?" affirms Baby Suggs's notion that loving one's self leads to freedom.

While Beloved represents the unchangeable nature of the past, Sethe, Paul D, and Denver embody and illustrate the possibilities of the present and future, as they evolve from slaves to free men and women. In the last section of the novel, Beloved is "broken up," and although the community has forgotten her, "occasionally, however, the rustle of a skirt hushes when they wake." As the novel closes with one word, "Beloved," Morrison seems to be challenging the reader not to forget.

Major Themes

Beloved's epigraph states "Sixty Million and more," referring to the estimated number of slaves who died on the Middle Passage. The narrative centers on Sethe, a former slave, and her struggle to move on from the past and to embrace her freedom. Morrison explores the lasting effects of slavery on individuals and society, the depths of a mother's love, and the power of community and memory. The novel also addresses black masculinity, spirituality, and the meaning of freedom.

Slavery and Freedom

While traditional slave narratives documented slaves' physical escape and their journeys to freedom, Morrison both revises and revives this structure as she depicts how slaves also survived psychological trauma. *Beloved* presents slavery as both an individual and a national trauma, exploring the damaging effects on characters who try to repress and then finally come to terms with their painful past.

Although Sethe is of the first generation to be freed, she and her children continue to live under slavery's destructive effects, and she works every day at "beating back the past." Morrison explores how slavery damages or prohibits a sense of self by depicting harrowing scenes in which slaves were treated as subhuman and traded as commodities. Though Paul D recalls that Mr. Garner called the slaves men, he now realizes the institution of slavery does not allow for "men." Under schoolteacher, Paul D was chained with a metal bit in his mouth and treated "less than a chicken sitting in the sun on a tub." The dehumanizing effects of the institution of slavery serve as the background of the novel and poison the memories of Sethe, who once heard schoolteacher giving his pupils a lesson on her "animal characteristics."

Morrison also describes the horrors of the Middle Passage. Beloved, possibly a survivor, recalls a "circle of iron" used to humiliate and physically control slaves. Baby Suggs, also a survivor of the Middle Passage, was moved from plantation to plantation, sold and resold, separated from all of her children, until she was placed at Sweet Home with her son. Slavery controlled identity and sexuality and robbed the slaves of their native African culture, as with Sethe's mother, who spoke in a dialect or language "which would never come back." *Beloved* explores the economic and sexual exploitation of slave women, and yet Morrison also shows how women, including Sethe and her mother, resisted this life-crippling institution.

The novel also depicts the horrors of slavery's aftereffects—the Ku Klux Klan, lynchings, whippings. For Stamp Paid, this history is symbolized in the ribbon he found in the water, "knotted around a curl of wet woolly hair, clinging to its bit of scalp." He carries it with him as an emblem and reminder of the terrible past. Other slaves faced insanity, suffering a complete loss of self. Sethe fears that she will also end her days clouded and claimed by mental illness. She succumbs temporarily to insanity when she kills her own daughter.

For Morrison, there are no clear words to describe slavery, only the "roaring" made up of "the mumbling of the black and angry dead" mixed in with "unspeakable thoughts, unspoken." Beloved embodies the collective pain and rage of the men and women who died on the Middle Passage. A haunting presence, she reminds the community of those untold stories of slavery.

Slavery affects not only the identities of its black victims but also those of the whites who perpetrate it. Though the supposedly enlightened Mr. Garner had "high principles," his position was still that of a slaveholder, and therefore he was part of the inhumane power structure that caused indescribable suffering. Sethe, Paul D, and Denver illustrate the possibilities of the future, as they evolve from slaves to individuals in full possession of their lives. Morrison suggests that our nation's identity, like the novel's characters, must be healed; otherwise, the country suffers a loss of humanity and compassion.

Maternal Love

The power of a mother's love for her children, a love that can conquer all, is another major theme in the novel. Sethe loves her children fiercely, with a "big" love. Slavery threatened to destroy the bonds between mothers and children. Sethe's tenuous relationship with her own mother, who was nearly a stranger to her, may also help to explain her own protective, needy love of her own children: "I know what it is to be without the milk that belongs to you; to have to fight and holler for it, and to have so little left."

When Sethe's milk for her children, a symbol of motherhood and nurturing, is taken from her, she is traumatized. She escapes Sweet Home not for her own freedom but because she wants to protect her children. Yet her love is "too thick" and causes her to kill her own daughter in order to "save" her from the horror of slavery. Paul D believes Sethe's immense love "was dangerous," but Stamp Paid defends Sethe: "She ain't crazy. She love those children." Sethe states that "thin love ain't love at all" and believes that her love "worked." But her love and excessive emotion also lead to destruction. When her murdered daughter returns, Sethe gives up and allows herself to be consumed. The strength of Sethe's love leads her almost to the point of death.

Beloved examines the power of motherly love—both the goodness and protection it offers and the "thick," excessive love that threatens destruction. Sethe's love for Beloved is like a desire for a life-sustaining substance: "I wouldn't draw breath without my children." Sethe wrongly believes that, with the return of Beloved, she has found peace. Her love for her children endures, but she does not find peace until she faces the painful past and the long shadows it has cast into her present life.

ERNEST J. GAINES

Biography

ERNEST J. GAINES was born on January 15, 1933, at the start of the Great Depression on the River Lake Plantation in Pointe Coupee Parish, Louisiana, to Manuel and Adrienne Gaines. His parents were sharecroppers on the same plantation where their family had been slaves. His father abandoned the family when Ernest was a young boy, and his mother was often away, looking for work. Gaines, the eldest of 12, was predominantly raised by his Aunt Augusteen. He attended school for the first six years on the plantation, where the students only went to classes for six months out of the year because they had to work in the fields picking cotton. He then spent three years at St. Augustine School, a Catholic school for African Americans.

When he was 15, Gaines moved to Vallejo, California, to join his mother and stepfather. He began spending most of his time at the library and wrote his first novel when he was 17, composing it on a typewriter his mother rented for him. He wrapped the manuscript in brown paper and sent it to a publisher in New York. When it was rejected, Gaines burned the manuscript.

He graduated high school in 1951 and began taking courses at Vallejo Junior College. Drafted by the U.S. Army in 1953, he spent two years as a soldier, then, with the help of the funds afforded him by the GI Bill, completed a bachelor's degree at San Francisco State College, where he published his first short story, "The Turtles," in a college magazine. He earned a degree in literature in 1957 and went on to study writing at Stanford University, receiving a prestigious Wallace Stegner fellowship. He published his first novel, *Catherine Carmier*, in 1964.

Gaines's books include *Mozart and Leadbelly: Stories and Essays* (2005), *A Gathering of Old Men* (1983), *In My Father's House* (1978), *A Long Day in November* (1971), *The Autobiography of Miss Jane Pittman* (1971), *Bloodline* (1968), and *Of Love and Dust* (1967). His 1993 novel, *A Lesson Before Dying*, won the

National Book Critics Circle Award for fiction and was nominated for the Pulitzer Prize. Gaines's fiction has been taught in high school and college classrooms and translated into many languages, including French, Spanish, German, Russian, and Chinese. Four of his works have been produced into television movies.

After the publication of *A Lesson Before Dying*, Gaines was awarded a prestigious MacArthur Foundation "genius grant." He was also inducted into the American Academy of Arts and Letters and the French Order of Arts and Letters as a Chevalier and awarded the National Humanities Medal the same year. Since 1984, Gaines has spent half of every year in San Francisco and the other half in Lafayette, Louisiana, where he teaches a creative writing workshop at the University of Louisiana.

Though his work is not strictly autobiographical, much of it resembles events from Gaines's life, and he has set some of his fiction on a Louisiana plantation similar to the place where he grew up. Gaines is known for his mastery of the first-person voice. In *The Autobiography of Miss Jane Pittman*, a 110-year-old narrator leads the reader on a journey through African-American history. He constructs narratives that document the lives of African Americans in the rural South. *A Lesson Before Dying* highlights the tensions that affected African Americans in the 1940s and reveals conflicts among African Americans, Creoles, and whites in a small town. Themes in Gaines's fiction include the construction of black masculinity, the destructive effects of racism, the valuable teachings of the elderly, alienation between fathers and sons, and the importance of familial and community roots.

The Autobiography of Miss Jane Pittman
Summary and Analysis

The novel begins with a note from the "editor," a local schoolteacher, who explains that he interviewed 110-year-old Jane Pittman in the beginning of 1962. Whenever her memory lapses, her friends fill in the details. "Miss Jane's story is all of their stories, and their stories are Miss Jane's," Gaines writes, a line that stresses the importance of community in the telling of African-American history. By establishing the story as an oral narrative, Gaines captures the authenticity of Jane's voice and recalls classic slave narratives that abolitionists used in the nineteenth century to influence public opinion about the horror of slavery. Miss Jane Pittman's story documents the African-American experience in the South from slavery to the civil rights movement.

The novel is divided into four books and subdivided into short chapters. The first book, "The War Years," begins with 10-year-old Jane (then called Ticey) living on a plantation somewhere in Louisiana during the Civil War. One day Union troops stop for water, and Colonel Brown converses with Ticey. He tells her that Ticey is a slave name and renames her Jane Brown. Jane thinks it is "the prettiest name I ever heard." When Jane refuses to answer to her slave name, her mistress beats her; this early act of defiance characterizes Jane's determination and her refusal to be oppressed. Renaming is a recurring motif in the novel. A year later, when the slaves are freed and the Civil War ends, many of them rename themselves, choosing Sherman or Lincoln to symbolize their freedom.

Jane leaves the plantation with a group led by Big Laura, but they are ambushed by the "patrollers," a group of racist, poor whites on horseback. Men on horseback, an emblem of the Old South, is a common image in the work; by connecting it to the patrollers, Gaines dispels myths of southern gallantry and depicts the true violence of racism. The patrollers massacre the just-freed slaves, including Big Laura and her baby, and only Jane and Ned, Big Laura's son, survive.

Jane sets out to find Colonel Brown, and the next six chapters document Jane and Ned's journey across Louisiana. Along the way, they encounter various characters, both black and white, who tell Jane that Ohio is too far and that she should go back to the plantation. One man offers a long-winded hypothesis on how long it will take Jane to reach Ohio (30 years), and Jane realizes "how wrong I had been for not listening to people," an early lesson on the importance of community. Though Jane remains sassy and outspoken, she starts to value others' thoughts and opinions.

When they arrive at a plantation run by Mr. Bone, he offers to pay Jane 10 dollars a month to work in the fields and provides schooling for Ned. Jane ends up staying for the next 10 or 12 years. In the beginning, life is good; however, the northerners essentially abandon the area, and the racist social order is reestablished. The original owner of the plantation, Colonel Dye, buys it back with money borrowed from northerners, and the quality of life for the African Americans living there severely diminishes: "It was slavery again, all right."

Time moves quickly in this section of the novel. Ned, 17, belongs to a committee that encourages blacks to flee to New Orleans, where they will be treated better. Threatened by the loss of the black workforce, the Ku Klux Klan comes "riding," looking for Ned, who is now like a son to Jane. If he does not leave, he will be killed. After his departure, Jane "cried all night." Jane cannot have children of her own but becomes a mother figure instead to many in the community.

After Ned leaves, Jane moves in with Joe Pittman, the love of her life. Independent and courageous, Joe refuses to stay on Dye's plantation, even though Dye demands that he pay him a large sum of money in order to leave. Joe comes up with the money, and he and Jane move to a ranch near the Texas–Louisiana border where Joe has found a job breaking horses. In this scene, the man-on-horseback motif represents Joe's courage and independence. They stay for 10 years and are happy there, until Jane grows increasingly afraid that Joe will be killed by a horse. She has a recurring dream about his death, and one day she sees a black stallion in the corral that resembles the horse from her dreams. A Creole woman tells Jane that Joe breaks horses in order to prove that he is a man; his skills win him respect from both black and white men. As a slave, Joe was denied his manhood; now he would rather lose his life than his respect. Jane tries to prevent his death by freeing the horse, but when Joe goes after it, he is killed by it; the stallion represents an untamed spirit that cannot be broken.

Unlike Jane, most of the male characters in the novel are not fully developed but carry important thematic weight in regard to issues of black manhood and freedom. When Ned returns with his family, Jane observes, "A boy had left here, a man had come back." After completing his education in Kansas, Ned returns to Louisiana to teach, and his lessons extend far beyond arithmetic and reading. Ned, the novel's first messianic figure, teaches Frederick Douglass's ideas on black justice and equality. In his sermon by the river, Ned wears his army uniform, asserting his identity as an American. The whites find him threatening and hire a Cajun, Albert Cluveau, to kill Ned. Though the community is afraid to support Ned, after he is killed, people are eager "to touch his body," reinforcing his portrayal as a Christlike figure.

Jane moves to Robert Samson's plantation in book 3, "The Plantation," which addresses the destructive forces of racism. The focus is no longer on Jane but on the plantation owners, Robert and his wife, Miss Amma Dean, and their son, Tee Bob. Robert has another son, Timmy, whose mother is a black woman living on the plantation. Though Timmy looks and acts more like Robert than Tee Bob does, Samson refuses to acknowledge him as his son and expects Timmy to act subservient to his half-brother. After Timmy gets into a fight with the white overseer, he must leave the plantation, and Tee Bob is heartbroken.

Years later, when Mary Agnes LeFabre, a light-skinned Creole, moves to the plantation to teach, Tee Bob falls in love with her. His friend Jimmy Caya warns him that "Africa is in her veins" and that she is there to be used for sex "and nothing else." Enraged by the comment, Tee Bob hits his friend. He asks Mary Agnes to run away with him to get married, but Mary Agnes, who understands "the rules," refuses: She tries to make him understand it is impossible to overturn or erase so many years of rigid social codes. When she offers herself sexually to him instead, he is devastated.

Trapped in the web of southern racism, Tee Bob feels there is no place for him, and he commits suicide. Representing a moral voice, a man named Jules Raynard stands up to Robert Samson, convincing him not to take revenge on Mary Agnes. Raynard holds the community responsble for Tee Bob's suicide: "We all killed him." Tee Bob is another Christ figure in the novel, dying for the sins of the whites.

In "The Quarters," the final book, Jane leaves the main house to move to the quarters with her people, a relocation that signals a shift in her role, as she becomes a vital part of the community she inhabits. This section focuses on Jimmy Aaron, the novel's most significant Christ figure. As a young boy, Jimmy, "the One," is raised by the community and listens to its stories about slavery. After the Supreme Court ruling on segregation (*Brown v. Board of Education*, 1954), Jimmy moves to New Orleans with his mother and becomes involved in the civil rights movement.

The civil rights movement threatened the social order that guaranteed white supremacy, and Robert Samson warns his tenants not to get involved. Jimmy returns and encourages the community to take a stand, but the people are old and afraid. Only Jane agrees to take part in Jimmy's political demonstration: He has planned for a black girl to drink from the town's water fountain designated for white use only, and after she is arrested, they will then march to the courthouse in protest.

On the day of the protest, more people from the plantation join Jane, and she cries from joy. When Robert Samson orders them all to go home because Jimmy has been killed, Jane insists "just a little piece of him is dead" and encourages everyone to continue on the march. Jane shows her courage as she walks past the plantation owner, asserting her freedom and equality.

Major Themes

The creation of Jane Pittman was inspired by Gaines's Aunt Augusteen Jefferson, a strong, determined woman to whom he dedicated the book. The novel tells the story of a woman achieving independence after being born into slavery, and it documents the history of the black experience in the American South. Gaines explores a population that was displaced at the end of the Civil War and reveals the strength of community and individual determination. Themes include the legacy of slavery and its effects on American society, the changes that courage and hope can bring, and the construction of black masculinity.

The Inheritance of Slavery

Even after the Civil War ends, the effects of slavery continue to dominate nearly every facet of southern society, personally marking Jane's life with brutality and oppression. After Big Laura and her baby are murdered by patrollers, Jane, numbed by the violence of slavery, cannot even cry. It is a system of inhumane oppression. One white woman wants Jane to come with her, promising her that she has always treated her slaves well. When Jane refuses, the woman cries from the realization that, even though she was "nice" to her slaves, she has been complicit in a brutal system.

Racist dynamics and attitudes are so ingrained in postwar southern society that some slaves do not know how to cope with freedom. Molly, for example, lived her entire life in a system that denied her independence, but when she is free, she is scared to leave her mistress. When she finally must go, she "died of a broken heart." Master-slave dynamics continue to influence the lives of the free, as evidenced in the way Timmy must ride his horse (symbolizing his manhood) behind his half-brother, Tee Bob, who rides a mule. On the plantation, which embodies and suggests the social order of the South, black women are exploited and expected to be submissive both emotionally and sexually. When Tee Bob falls in love with Mary Agnes, viewing her as a human being instead of an object, he challenges and upsets this system.

The African Americans living on Samson's plantation endure injustices because they are afraid to speak out. The effects of slavery run deep, and "the mark of fear," Jane explains, "is not easily removed." When individuals such as Tee Bob, Ned Douglass, and Jimmy Aaron defy these social codes left over from slavery, they end up dead for threatening or upending the established social order. Although great strides are made throughout Jane's lifetime, at the end of her life, she is still living on a plantation, a strong symbol of the legacy of slavery in the South.

Courageous Sacrifice

Characters perform large and small acts of courage in the novel, from renaming themselves to sacrificing their lives, in order to bring about social change. Both Ned and Jimmy are willing to die for the rights of their people. Ned, asserting his independence and freedom, teaches these values to others and thus poses a threat to a racist social system that is dependent on ignorance. When Ned gives a sermon about what it means to be a free black American, armed white men watch his every move. Ned's courage affects the children, who watch their teacher closely. When Ned is shot by Albert Cluveau, Ned refuses to crawl, choosing to die with courage. On the other hand, Albert is a coward and dies a painful, lonely death.

At the time, the community was too scared to stand behind Ned, but solidarity is necessary for real change to be enacted. Like Ned before him, Jimmy is a leader, uniting the people who are ready to take a stand. Years after Ned's sacrifice, Jimmy inspires the community to fight the racist system they have inhabited all of their lives. However, he is killed for his courage.

Though Jane is not a civil rights leader like Jimmy, her own courage motivates and unifies the others. Jane refuses to internalize society's racism and demands to be treated like a human being and not like "a dog." At the end of her life, she stands up to Robert Samson. It is clear that he no longer holds power over her as she walks past him, now seeing him as "Robert" instead of "Mr. Samson"; the shift in the name she calls him reveals that she sees herself as equal to him and is no longer afraid. The community follows her lead, and it is their courage, a catalyst for change, that helps to dismantle the town's Jim Crow laws.

A Lesson Before Dying
Summary and Analysis

A Lesson Before Dying revolves around two African-American men who teach each other how to attain dignity and manhood in a society that is steeped in a legacy of more than 300 years of racism. The action takes place in 1948 on a plantation near Bayonne, Louisiana. The town is representative of the Deep South in the1940s and 1950s, a society that has barely altered its racial attitudes since the abolition of slavery.

The novel opens in late October, during the sugarcane harvest. The protagonist, Grant Wiggins, narrates the story in the first person, starting off by adopting a distant, journalistic tone. Jefferson is a young black man accused of murder. Though Grant does not attend his trial, he is able to describe the scene: "I was not there, yet I was there. No, I did not go to the trial, I did not hear the verdict, because I knew all the time what it would be." He is not surprised by the outcome of the trial, not because Jefferson is guilty but because of the racist legal system.

Jefferson claims he tagged along with two black men on a trip to a liquor store. The men got into an argument with the white store owner, and gunfire was exchanged. Everyone, except for Jefferson, is killed. Instead of fleeing, Jefferson stayed at the scene of the crime. The jury, made up of 12 white men, sentence Jefferson to death. As a black man, Jefferson not only is denied justice but also stripped of his humanity. His own lawyer relies on racist language and argues that there is no point in executing Jefferson because it would be like executing a hog.

Upon hearing these words, Miss Emma, Jefferson's godmother, is determined that Jefferson learn that he is valued as a human being: "I don't want them to kill no hog. I want a man to go to that chair, on his own two feet." Miss Emma and Grant's Aunt Lou, also called Tante Lou, enlist Grant to teach Jefferson the truth. Grant is university educated, a proud black man struggling to live in a society that denies his status and compromises his identity as a man. He deplores the injustices that the black community suffers, but he feels powerless to change things: "I teach what the white folks around here tell me to teach." He does not want this job, but he cannot refuse his aunt or Miss Emma, described as "boulders," in reference to their strength and resolve. These older women have lived all of their lives under the oppression of the South, but it is their hope that the younger generations will experience change. Though Grant is often rude to or dismissive of his aunt, she exerts a moral pull over him.

One of Grant's main conflicts is with himself. Though he returned to the tiny plantation to teach, he feels trapped. He states, "I hated this place," and "I hated teaching." He wants to remove himself from the racism of the South but stays because of Vivian, the only person who makes him happy. A light-skinned Creole schoolteacher who was rejected by her family for associating with darker-skinned blacks, Vivian is still married to another man and is the mother of two young children. At first, when Tante Lou and Miss Emma meet Vivian, they are distrustful, but they grow to respect her. A source of love and strength, Vivian is both Grant's link to the future and his anchor to the community.

Grant, who grew up on Pichot's Plantation, is well aware of the unspoken rules about race, and he feels resentful of the master-servant dynamics still in place. His sense of dignity and identity are compromised when he must enter Pichot's house through the servants' door, then wait for two and a half hours in the kitchen for Sheriff Guidry and Henry Pichot. He feels humiliated each time he visits the prison, where he is scrutinized by the sheriff, trying to "break me down to the nigger I was born to be." For years his aunt Lou spared Grant this kind of humiliation by sending him off to school: She taught him that he is a man and nothing less and now wants him to extend the lesson to Jefferson.

In the classroom, Grant is distant and unsympathetic toward the children. He worries that his own former teacher, Matthew Antoine, a racist light-skinned Creole, was correct when he said there was no point in teaching black children because their only future is to work the fields. Grant's powerlessness is heightened when the white superintendent visits. Instead of answering Grant's questions about the lack of books and supplies, the superintendent inspects the students' hands and teeth like a slave master, reinforcing the racist belief that black children do not need an education.

Similarly, Jefferson also feels angry and trapped. In prison for a crime he did not participate in, he withdraws from his visitors and refuses to eat Miss Emma's food. Barely literate, docile, and believing himself to be expendable, Jefferson has slowly been ground down by the racist stereotypes that dominated the world in which he was raised. He has taken the lawyer's words to heart. When Grant visits, Jefferson gets down on all fours and sniffs and nuzzles the bag of food in imitation of a hog, an action that reveals how hurt and angered he was by the lawyer's words. Jefferson does not know how to express his feelings; his lack of voice contributes to his feelings of isolation and worthlessness.

Grant's early attempts at conversation with Jefferson are trivial and half-hearted, but he is sensitive to Miss Emma's pain, and on the next visit, he tells Jefferson that he must stop hurting her. Jefferson responds by making a crude comment about Vivian, but even though Grant is insulted, he does not succumb to anger and feels only sympathy for Jefferson.

The sheriff wants Jefferson to remain docile and subservient and considers Grant's visits a waste of time; Grant silently agrees that he has not "done a thing" to help the prisoner. Both the sheriff and Pichot represent white authority figures who desire to keep blacks "in their place." The only sympathetic white character is Paul, a prison guard who converses with Grant and shows concern for Jefferson. Paul challenges the great divide that exists between the black and white communities.

At the Christmas play, Grant still stands apart from the community, but he is less cynical, and his description of the community reveals his deep love for the people. Throughout the novel, Grant expresses his desire to run away with Vivian and leave everything behind, but Vivian knows "You love them more than you hate this place."

The pace of the novel becomes more urgent after the execution date is set for the second Friday after Easter. On Grant's fourth visit, for the first time Jefferson starts to talk to him. Jefferson tells him he wants a gallon of vanilla ice cream for his final meal. Slowly, Jefferson ends his isolation. He engages in conversation, asks after others, and expresses gratitude when Grant brings him a radio, a notebook, and pecans from the children. When Grant calls him "partner," he opens the door to friendship.

The next time that Miss Emma, Tante Lou, and Reverend Ambrose visit, however, Jefferson again withdraws. In one of the novel's most moving scenes, Grant walks around the dayroom with him and gives a speech on the meaning of a hero as someone who does something for others. Grant admits that he is not a hero: "I want to live for myself and for my woman and for nobody else." In this speech, in which he "speak[s] from the heart," Grant faces his own weaknesses and also "touche[s] something deep down" in Jefferson, who begins to cry. When Grant sits down and eats gumbo with the others, it is a small action that represents a major change in his view of himself as a human being.

At the Rainbow Club, Grant is provoked into a fight with two biracial brick-layers who make rude comments about Jefferson. The fight symbolizes Grant's physical response to racism and his growing commitment to Jefferson. Vivian takes care of Grant, but she wants more from him, challenging him to give his best. He has used Vivian as an escape from his problems, instead of facing the reality of their lives together. He starts to leave but looks outside and realizes that there is nothing for him out there without her. He returns and rests his head in her lap, a sign of his growing openness and vulnerability.

Reverend Ambrose, Miss Emma, and Tante Lou are concerned about the state of Jefferson's soul, but when they ask Grant to talk to Jefferson, Grant refuses. He feels that the church has given an inadequate response to the injustice the black community has suffered, and he can barely hide his contempt for Reverend Ambrose. In an important lesson for Grant, Reverend Ambrose accuses Grant of not knowing himself or his community. He explains that sometimes in order to relieve pain, a person must lie: "They sent you to school to relieve pain, to relieve hurt—and if you have to lie to do it, then you lie."

In the beginning, Grant is a poor teacher, he is rude to Lou and Miss Emma, and he is full of anger. Yet, all along he has known that Lou and Emma want someone to be proud of, so he puts his faith in Jefferson and feels confident that he will prove racism's lie in portraying Jefferson's life as expendable. Grant tells him, "Yes, we all need you. Every last one of us."

Jefferson emerges in the novel as a messianic or savior figure and a mobilizing force who brings the community together. He realizes he has a place in the community and finds his voice in his diary, which is presented in a stream-of-consciousness style. The misspellings and grammatical errors add a realistic tone of raw intimacy, bringing the readers into Jefferson's mind as he grapples with the fact that he will die. He considers serious questions, observes the beauty found around him, and feels loved by the community. The diary also reveals how Grant arranged visits from the students and the elders and testifies to the strong friendship between the men.

On the morning of the execution, the actions of the citizens, both black and white, are reported in a journalistic style. Because the execution is performed locally, the entire community is affected. As the black community refuses to work that day, the whites, who depend on the labor, cannot ignore what is happening. Jefferson has begun to change the lives of those around him. Even the sheriff shows him respect, and on the day of the execution, he tells his wife that "he wished this day had never gotten here."

Grant does not attend the execution, but Reverend Ambrose is there: "that old man is much braver than I." At noon, the hour of the execution, Grant instructs his students to get on their knees, then he walks outside, feeling confused and sad. He knows he should have gone to the execution and berates himself: "Why wasn't I standing beside him? Why wasn't my arm around him? Why? Why wasn't I back there with the children?" When he sees a yellow butterfly, a symbol of life and change, he knows that the execution is over.

Paul arrives with Jefferson's diary and affirms that Jefferson was the strongest man in the room: "And straight he walked." In the parting scene, Paul holds Grant's hands, saying, "Allow me to be your friend," signaling that the divide between white and black can be overcome through friendship and understanding. Grant, no longer emotionally isolated, goes in to face the children, and for the first time, with his heart fully opened, he cries. Grant has changed by allowing himself to feel emotions and by reaching out to others, while Jefferson is not rendered anonymous by his execution, having been transformed into a compassionate and dignified human being.

Major Themes

A Lesson Before Dying is a powerful exploration of race, injustice, and manhood. Gaines reveals the prevalence of racism in society, from the penal system to the schools, and exposes racial myths that dominated southern society after World War II. The novel explores relationships between the generations and among the races and explores what it means to be a hero. Two crucial themes are the achievement of a black male identity and the power of community.

Black Male Identity

The novel examines how black men can attain manhood in a society that once considered them to be "three-fifths human." Grant explains that 300 years of oppression have affected black men's perception of themselves, leaving them "broken." He fears that undoing the effects of so many years of oppression is impossible, but Miss Emma wants Jefferson to walk, not crawl to the whites executing him, because "she knows that she will never get another chance to see a black man stand for her."

Jefferson and Grant are opposites in many ways, yet equally degraded by racism; they must learn how to attain the male identity that society has tried to deny them. Grant will receive his lessons from the community, learning at the Rainbow Club, his aunt's house, the prison, and the classroom, while Jefferson learns his lessons behind bars. Grant fully inhabits his manhood by becoming more selfless and vulnerable. In the beginning, Grant wonders if it is better that Jefferson die in ignorance: "Why not let the hog die without knowing anything?" But as Grant develops into a more compassionate human being, he challenges Jefferson to defy racist stereotypes: "You can prove them wrong."

At first, Jefferson takes the lawyer's words to heart, that he is as expendable as a hog. He refuses to interact with his visitors, stares at the walls, and will not eat the food his godmother cooks for him. With Grant's help, however, he transforms. In the end, he stands up straight, gratefully accepts the nourishment his godmother provides, and engages in conversation. He challenges Grant and explores his own ideas as they discuss heaven, God, and manhood. He is no longer thinking only of himself but shows concern for others.

Jefferson chooses to die with dignity. He takes a hot shower with a new bar of soap and eats a last meal cooked by Miss Emma. Instead of the gallon of ice cream, Jefferson wants a small portion in a cup. He stays awake all night to watch his last sunrise. Though he is shaking, he is courageous and grateful, and in the end, he faces his unjust death with bravery and with his dignity intact. Jefferson's attainment of manhood is symbolic, a way "to change this vicious cycle."

Community Versus Isolation

The community is divided between blacks and whites and, within the black community, divisions arise between dark-skinned blacks and light-skinned Creoles. Yet, because of Jefferson, the divisions become less rigid. The black community especially grows closer as it provides its strong support. When Grant buys Jefferson a radio, he borrows the money from a couple of bar owners in the black community. When the date for Jefferson's execution is set, the community descends on Miss Emma to show their support and sympathy.

The two main characters start out as isolated, and by the end, they are stronger because they have engaged and joined the community. In the beginning, Grant's feelings of powerlessness and his pride cause him to be emotionally alienated from the community. Reverend Ambrose accuses Grant of thinking only of himself and tells him, "You don't even know yourself." Though Grant is university educated, he must be educated by his community in order to learn about himself. Reverend Ambrose speaks of the pain his Aunt Lou has gone though, but Grant has never noticed the scars on her knees: "And that's the difference between me and you, boy. . . . I know my people." Over the course of the novel, Grant becomes more concerned with the individual lives that make up the community and realizes that he is a "part of the whole."

Jefferson also slowly lets go of his isolation by asking after others, eating his godmother's food, and engaging in conversation. He receives many visitors including the children and the elders. When the mentally challenged boy Bok gives him a marble, he accepts the gift with gratitude. Though Jefferson must die, the novel ends in hope. The children, who have brought Jefferson gifts, are the future of the community, and they have shown only goodness, love, and truth. Jefferson's death affects everyone in town—white, black, Creole. The entire black community comes together because of his courage; through him, they can realize their own self-worth.

WALTER DEAN MYERS

Biography

WALTER DEAN MYERS was born Walter Milton Myers on August 12, 1937, in West Virginia. After his mother died when he was three years old, he was raised by the Dean family in Harlem, New York City. Myers experienced a happy childhood but was conscious of his speech impediment. Unable to communicate well orally, he turned to writing poetry and short stories and acquired an early love of reading.

Discouraged that his family was too poor to send him to college, Myers quit high school and joined the army in 1954. After, he held various jobs, including working for the New York State Department of Labor and the post office. Myers married Joyce Smith in 1960 and had two children; they divorced in 1970. During this time, Myers wrote nonfiction and stories and sent out his work to various magazines. The turning point in his career came in 1969 when he won a contest run by the Council on Interracial Books for Children with his book *Where Does a Day Go?*

Myers married Constance Brendel in 1973, and they had a son. He worked as an editor for a publishing company for seven years, and when he was laid off, he decided to try to make a living by writing full time. Myers also continued his education; more than two decades after leaving high school, he graduated from Empire State College. Now a father of three and a grandfather, Myers lives in Jersey City, New Jersey.

Since the publication of his first children's book, Myers has published more than 80 works, including young adult novels, biographies, historical fiction, poetry, fables, picture books, ghost stories, and adventure stories. One of today's most renowned young adult authors, Myers is a five-time recipient of the Coretta Scott King Award, winner of the first Michael L. Printz Award, and a recipient of the Margaret A. Edwards Award for lifetime achievement. Two of his works have also been named Newbery Honor Books.

In 1975, Myers published his first young adult novel, *Fast Sam, Cool Clyde and Stuff*, one of the first books for this age group to focus on African-American urban youth. Myers is known best for his realistic young adult novels that take place in Harlem, including *Scorpions* (1988), *Monster* (1999), and *Autobiography of My Dead Brother* (2005), among many others. Other popular and critically acclaimed novels include *The Glory Field* (1994), *Shooter* (2004), and *Fallen Angels* (1988), which has made the American Library Association's list of frequently challenged books due to profanity and its realistic depictions of the Vietnam War.

Myers's young adult novels tend to focus on teens struggling to grow up in a world touched by gang life, drug use, violence, and peer pressure. Despite the bleak situations, Myers's message is positive: Young people must persevere and believe in themselves. Recurring themes and motifs in his work include father-son relationships, discovering one's self, friendship, and black masculinity. In many of his books, the protagonist, a young African-American male, faces dangerous influences and temptations and must make tough choices. Although the characters confront difficult issues, whether on the streets of Harlem or the battlefields of Vietnam, Myers's novels also stress themes of survival, pride, and hope.

Fallen Angels

Summary and Analysis

Fallen Angels (1988) describes the horrors of the Vietnam War from the perspective of Richie Perry, a 17-year-old African-American male from Harlem. Told in the first-person perspective, the novel is both about Vietnam and Perry's coming of age.

The Vietnam War, which lasted from 1959 to 1973, was a controversial conflict. The United States's involvement in the conflict was hotly debated on many fronts. The United States reached its highest level of involvement in the war in approximately 1967, the year in which *Fallen Angels* is set. Richie enlists in the army because, although he is smart and ambitious, he cannot afford college and wants to leave Harlem. The army is also a way for him to earn money to send home to his single mother and his little brother, Kenny. Perry used to dream of becoming a writer "like James Baldwin," but the reality is bleak: For a young black man growing up in Harlem in the 1960s, there were very few opportunities.

The novel opens with Perry on a flight to Vietnam where he meets Judy Duncan, a nurse from Texas, and Harold "Peewee" Gates, a high school dropout from Chicago, who handles himself by making brash jokes and provoking others. Like

Peewee, Perry still holds onto many illusions about the military, including his belief that a knee injury in the past will be sufficient cause to prevent him from entering combat. After a series of minor mishaps regarding their arrival, he begins to question the military's reputation for competence and efficiency.

Perry is also surprised that "there were a lot of black guys." During the Vietnam era, the majority of soldiers were working class, and many also came from minority populations, in contrast to the college students (many of whom were middle class and white) who were exempt from the draft. Ironically, many men who were fighting to defend American values faced some of the greatest obstacles preventing them from achieving the American Dream. Peewee, who grew up poor, likes the army because "anything anybody got in the army, I got. You got a gun, I got a gun. You got boots, I got boots." Peewee and Perry spit on their hands and shake, a sign of their loyalty to each other and of their boyish idealism.

Perry and Peewee are assigned to the Alpha Company, transferred to Chu Lai, and told that their work will be "light stuff." They meet some of the other soldiers, and Peewee immediately provokes Johnson, a large African-American man from Savannah, Georgia, who is the squad's machine gunner. They also meet Sergeant Simpson, nearing the end of his duty; Monaco, a "sweet-faced Italian kid," who takes the dangerous position as point man; Brew, who is religious and plans to join the ministry; and Corporal Brunner, who is highly respectful to those above him in rank but bullies those below him.

After their first patrol, a mine goes off, killing a new recruit. Jenkins's death makes an impact on Perry, who begins to realize that the threat of death is never far away. Perry's and the others' fears are somewhat alleviated, however, by their youth and naiveté, and they take false comfort in the peace talks in Paris, believing soon they will be sent to Hawaii. Much of their time is spent waiting around for something to happen. They play ping-pong, write letters, drink beer, get into arguments, and listen to the news, trying to create a sense of normalcy. The threat of danger presents itself in many forms: malaria, venereal diseases, and Viet Cong uprisings, not to mention environmental factors such as mosquitoes, rats, and the difficult climate and terrain.

As the soldiers adjust to this setting, the people who are still in the "World," as it is called, continue to go on with their lives. One day Peewee receives a letter from his girlfriend telling him that she has married another man in his absence. When Perry tries to write letters home, they seem dishonest. It is difficult for Perry to share with Kenny and his mother the realities of war, as his illusions about heroism and the dignity of war begin to dissipate.

Lobel, whose uncle is a Hollywood movie director, attempts to uphold such illusions by describing the war as a movie. He warns Perry "you're really hooked on reality. It's a bad scene." When a Viet Cong soldier is killed, Perry does not look at him and tries to find comfort in Lobel's illusion: "It wasn't real . . . maybe it was just some kind of movie." However, Perry's illusions are shattered when he is on a mission with the Charlie Company, and the platoon mistakenly shoots and kills at least 15 of their own men. Perry and the others are stunned by the chaos and senseless deaths.

Perry is thoughtful, curious, and compassionate. One reason he joined the army was "to get away from all the questions" about his future and who he is. Now he still does not know what his future holds, realizing that the army will not provide the answers. However, he recalls the words of his teacher Mrs. Liebow, "You're too young to be just an observer in life," and begins to take an active role in discovering himself.

The soldiers are sent into villages to befriend the locals and lure them away from the Viet Cong by distributing malaria pills, bandages, chocolate bars, and C-rations. Perry is disturbed that they must convince them that the U.S. soldiers are "the good guys." He still holds onto the belief that there is a clear line between good and bad and that he is on the right side.

During a major battle, the squad's leader, Lieutenant Carroll, a gentle, kind man, is killed, and the soldiers, overcome by grief, react by shooting at the village. This is a turning point in the novel: "Lieutenant Carroll's death was close. It hung around our shoulders and filled the spaces between us." Perry begins to seriously search for answers. He realizes the line between good and bad is ambiguous and longs to find meaning amid the chaos of war.

The soldiers talk about the draft, and Brunner expresses his anger at the antiwar demonstrators. The soldiers in Vietnam did not have the overwhelming support of the population at home, and many received expressions of contempt from the public when they returned. The young men do not yet realize how popular the antiwar movement is and believe they will be treated like heroes when they return. In addition to controversy about the war, racial tensions were also escalating across the United States, which the soldiers do not discuss.

By now, the soldiers realize they will not be going home anytime soon. As the fighting increases, the sounds of war become "a constant thing." On another patrol, the company's new leader, Gearhart, makes a mistake and lights a flare, exposing them. Later, Simpson informs Perry that he had set up the mines facing the wrong way: His mistake could have killed them all. The war is no longer a distant thing: "We were in the middle of it, and it was deeply within us."

They return to a village whose inhabitants had been massacred by the Viet Cong. Perry feels powerless: "I wanted to fire my weapon, to destroy the nightmare around me. I didn't want it to be real, this much death, this much dying, this waste of human life." Perry worries that the U.S. soldiers are not all that different from the enemy: "We could have killed as easily as we mourned. We could have burned as easily as we put out the fires." When a Viet Cong soldier pulls a gun on him, Perry kills a man for the first time. Back at the base, he grapples with his own ability to kill and begins to cry. Peewee holds him until they fall asleep.

The company is transferred to "the deep boonies," a remote place without protection. On one of their first missions they are hunkered down in the pitch black, when a leech lands on Perry's hand, scaring him before he realizes what it is. When they hear the Viet Cong soldiers, Perry is ready to squeeze the trigger, but Gearhart does not give the orders because there are too many of them, and the American soldiers would have been outgunned and overwhelmed in the skirmish.

Meanwhile, Captain Stewart, who is only concerned with his promotion, continues to volunteer Alpha Company on every mission possible; he also inflates the number of Viet Cong who were killed in his reports to the media and pressures Simpson to extend his service. During a battle, both Perry and Brew are shot. Brew dies, but Perry wakes up in a medical center, where he sees Judy Duncan again. He was hit by shrapnel but is able to return to duty. Feeling psychologically unable to face any more combat, Perry panics and considers going AWOL but then returns to his platoon, his duty stripping him of the desire to assert control over his own life.

Simpson goes back to the "World," and the new sergeant Dongan proves to be racist, putting the black soldiers in the most dangerous positions. The soldiers, both black and white, deeply bond nonetheless. The horrors they have witnessed unite them and bring them closer. In one harrowing scene, a Vietnamese woman hands her child, rigged with a landmine, to an American solider; the child blows up in his hands. Peewee is making a doll for the woman's children, and after the explosion, the doll "lay face down in the endless mud," symbolizing the horror and violence of a war in which children are blown up.

Tensions increase between the American soldiers and their Vietnamese allies in a battle in which Perry's company climbs a hill to try to draw fire. They return to regroup then climb the hill again, this time with the Vietnamese soldiers in the lead. When the enemy attacks, many of the Vietnamese allies are killed. Dongan is also killed, and Perry kills a young enemy solider who "looked scared and tired, the same as me." The horrific events continue when they must burn the bodies of their fellow soldiers so that they will not be violated by the Viet Cong. When Perry looks at them, he considers his own mortality: "I was afraid of the dead guys. . . . They were me." They burn the bodies but forget to take the dog tags to identify the men, an action that stresses the anonymity of war: Despite the myths of the heroic soldiers, many are killed in obscurity. Perry wants to describe what the war is really like, and he finally writes a truthful letter to Kenny: "the war was about us killing people and about people killing us, and I couldn't see much more to it."

With Brunner as the squad leader, they go to patrol a river where Viet Cong activity is suspected. When enemy soldiers start shooting at the men,

Peewee and Perry get separated from their squad and run to the top of a ridge. They peek out and realize that an entire battalion of North Vietnamese has been patrolling the river. They hide in a spider hole or small bunker and, in the morning, when a Viet Cong soldier checks the hole, they kill him. They head back to the landing site and see Monaco by a tree, looking terrified because the enemy has him surrounded. When the chopper arrives, Peewee and Richie bravely open fire, alerting the choppers.

Both Richie and Peewee are wounded in the chaos. At the medical center, Monaco tells them they saved his life, but Perry realizes "We're all dead and just hoping that we come back to life when we get into the World again." He is saddened to find out that the nurse Judy Duncan was killed when her field hospital was bombed.

Perry's medical profile is finally processed, and Peewee's wounds are serious enough that he is discharged. As they are leaving, the new recruits arrive, and though Peewee and Perry try to be hopeful, they feel beaten down: "We were tired of this war." The contrast between the new recruits and the exhausted soldiers reveals the suffering that the new recruits will likely encounter. Still, Peewee and Perry do not escape the constant presence of death. They fly home on the same plane that is carrying the caskets of dead soldiers. They are not excited but numb, even scared on the journey home. A passenger complains about the wine, reminding them of the triviality they will have to readjust to as they gather their strength and make the transition back to the "World."

Major Themes

Fallen Angels was named an ALA Best Book for Young Adults and received the Parents' Choice Award and the Coretta Scott King Award. Myers wrote the book as a tribute to his younger brother, who was killed in Vietnam; the loss of his brother deeply affected Myers's views on war. Myers undercuts the illusions of war as heroic and purposeful with a strong antiwar message and addresses such issues as racial discrimination and prejudices within the military. The novel is also about coming of age, friendship, and the loss of innocence.

Overcoming Prejudice

As the civil rights movement gained momentum, the 1960s were a time of hope, change, and racial tension. Myers depicts how this racial tension affected the army ranks but was often overcome as soldiers from different races and backgrounds lived with one another, fighting in battles together and often forming close friendships.

In the beginning, racial tension and prejudices flare up often among the Alpha squad. The soldiers use racial slurs and derogatory language, and these incidents often lead to physical fights. There is also racism directed at the Vietnamese.

The soldiers try to distance themselves from the enemy forces by dehumanizing them, but when Brunner uses the derogatory term *gooks*, Johnson compares it to an equally derogatory word directed at blacks.

As war takes its toll, the bond between the soldiers deepens; friendship provides some sense of meaning in the war. The soldiers' camaraderie and friendships also help them to overcome their prejudices. Gearhart, for example, admits to Perry that he "never thought much about black people before I got into the army," but now he feels close to the soldiers, black and white. Even the white members are outraged by Dongan's racism. Lobel says he will side with the black soldiers against Dongan, and Monaco also displays his loyalty. Furthermore, Johnson tells Richie that he does not care about Lobel's sexual orientation, claiming that any soldier who fights with him is an ally. The squad members support one another, despite their differences; their youth and loss of innocence ultimately bond them more than any racial, ethnic, or socioeconomic similarities.

Myths of War

Myers depicts how the young men arrive in Vietnam with illusions of heroics, dignity, and purpose but eventually discover only meaninglesness. When a television crew asks why they are fighting, the soldiers give stock responses, holding up ideals about defending freedom and democracy. They eventually realize they are fighting only to stay alive.

Lobel's description of Hollywood war movies and the heroes they portray only further highlights the stark reality of their situation, in which men die in obscurity and chaos. The myths of heroism make it difficult for Perry to write truthful letters to his family. Instead, he tries to protect them from the reality, as he does with Lieutenant Carroll's wife; Perry writes a letter to her that upholds the myth of heroism and evokes confidence in the purpose of the war and the army.

Yet the reality is that the young, "the angel warriors," are fighting the wars waged by the older leaders and losing their innocence as they face unspeakable horrors. Perry grapples with ideas of good and evil and longs to find meaning, but over and over he is faced with only chaos and senselessness. After members of a U.S. platoon accidentally kill some of their own men, Perry understands that the soldiers "died because somebody else was scared, maybe careless. They died because they were in Nam, where being scared made you do things you would regret later. We were killing our brothers, ourselves." Perry attempts to cling to the idea that they are good, but he notices how the villagers fear them, like "the bad guys [riding] into town." After Carroll is killed, old men and women run for their lives, and Perry's illusions about being the good guys who protect the Vietnamese are further dispelled: "These were the people we had come to save, to pacify. Now it was ourselves that we were saving."

Perry realizes his return and re-entry to normal society will not be easy because the "World" is protected from the reality of war, symbolized by the newspaper articles that sanitize the war by naming battles but not describing the lives lost. Before he arrived in Vietnam, "All I had thought about combat was that I would never die, that our side would win, and that we would all go home somehow satisfied. And now all the dying around me, and all the killing, was making me look at myself again, hoping to find something more than the kid I was." By the time he returns home, he is no longer an innocent kid; he has witnessed violence and death and learned many hard truths about the world.

Monster
Summary and Analysis

In *Monster*, a coming-of-age tale, the protagonist, 16-year-old Steve Harmon, is on trial in New York City and could face the death penalty or at the very least be sentenced to 25 years in prison for his alleged participation in a drugstore robbery that ended in murder. The basic facts of the case emerge: A drugstore on 145th Street in Harlem was robbed, and the West Indian owner, 55-year-old Alguinaldo Nesbitt, was shot to death. Two men were seen entering the store: James King, 23, and Richard "Bobo" Evans, 22. Steve's alleged role was to serve as a lookout.

The novel examines both the consequences of the young yielding to temptation and the flaws of the American justice system. Myers compassionately depicts how Steve, a naive teenager, is caught up in the violent circumstances of an adult world. Steve's fear and vulnerability are made evident in the opening lines: "The best time to cry is at night, when the lights are out and someone is being beaten up and screaming for help." At the detention center, Steve quickly learns not to let others see him cry. He lives under the fear of rape and physical abuse and feels demoralized by the way he must live under the constant gaze of other prisoners and guards. Steve's world has been turned upside down: "If your life outside was real, then everything in here is just the opposite."

The situation is so frightening that, to distance himself, Steve views the events as if he were directing a movie. The beginning chapter uses text styles that resemble the opening credits of a movie. In Mr. Sawicki's film class at Stuyvesant High School, Steve learned that a film should not be predictable, so in the imagined film that portrays and relates his experiences, Steve never reveals the full story but challenges the reader to determine his guilt or innocence. By employing this film device, Myers is able to depict the courtroom drama by focusing mainly on dialogue and action and present the information to the reader in nearly the same way it is being presented at the trial. However, the readers are also privy to flashbacks and to Steve's handwritten journal entries that reveal his raw emotions and add intimacy to the narrative.

The bored-looking judge and the attorneys are white and the defendants are African American, a circumstance that possibly contributes to Steve's feeling of powerlessness. Steve's lawyer, Kathy O'Brien, is direct and businesslike but also tries to encourage Steve to view his situation as positively as possible. Despite her support, however, O'Brien never says if she believes that Steve is innocent, and this troubles him. O'Brien wants to make Steve into "a human being in the eyes of the jury," to undo the prosecutor Sandra Petrocelli's definition of him as a "monster." Myers raises questions about the justice system and its treatment of youth by showing how a teenaged boy is portrayed as a ruthless criminal. That Steve titles his movie *Monster* reveals how deeply the prosecutor's words impact him. Steve is terrified that he no longer knows who he is: "I see a face looking back at me but I don't recognize it." The experience strips him of his self-respect and independence. One of the main themes is Steve's coming of age and his struggle to rediscover himself. Myers depicts Steve as a sympathetic but flawed character, highlighting his immaturity and youth.

Two Riker's Island inmates testify for the prosecution; the men struck deals with the district attorney to provide information in exchange for a shorter sentence or early release. Steve sits by quietly, powerless and silenced as his future is being determined. Flashbacks periodically interrupt the courtroom scenes to reveal additional details about Steve's life and background. We learn that when he was 12, he threw a rock that unintentionally struck a woman. Instead of apologizing, Steve ran, and the woman's date hit his friend Tony as a result. This scene suggests that Steve may have a history of ducking from responsibility but also portrays the prevalence of violence in the neighborhood. Another flashback shows Steve hanging out with the accused James King and a few other neighborhood residents. Their poverty and the overwhelming feeling of their lack of personal power drive the conversation. King talks about getting a crew together to pull a robbery, his macho posturing creating the illusion of authority and leadership.

Steve continues to feel disconnected from the trial: "It's like the lawyers and the judge and everybody are doing a job that involves me, but I don't have a role." His lack of power haunts him even in his sleep, as he dreams that he is in court asking questions but "nobody could hear me." Steve's fear and anguish are starkly contrasted to the glib, friendly conversations among the judge, lawyers, and officers. Even though they may be on different sides, their lives are not dramatically affected by the case, and they possess a freedom that Steve has had stripped from him.

Though the main thrust of the novel is the psychological drama of Steve's situation, Myers also examines the powerlessness of young black men within the justice system. It is evident, for example, that the police did not put time into the investigation; instead of dusting for fingerprints, they looked to strike deals with inmates. Also, Steve was treated like a monster from the moment of his arrest, when a detective said that he would be happy if Steve received the death penalty. Furthermore, the legal punishment for the crime, if Steve indeed played a role, seems extreme in relation to his level of involvement.

Myers develops Steve's character by contrasting him with the other characters. Osvaldo Cruz is a tough 14-year-old gang member. A flashback portrays Osvaldo as a bully taunting Steve: "You might be hanging out with some people, but when the deal goes down, you won't be around." Osvaldo represents the young, powerless male who, pressured by his surroundings, falls into a life of violence and crime. Myers portrays the environment that the boys grew up in as a place where crime is common and there is a pressure for young boys to act tough. Steve wanted to impress the others with his toughness but now fears the jury will see him and Osvaldo as the same person. Steve's sensitivity is displayed when he is upset by the photographs of the murdered Mr. Nesbitt; similarly, when Steve learns that Nesbitt "drowned in his own blood," Steve "catches his breath sharply," while King appears indifferent.

Steve believes in himself, even though his self-esteem continues to diminish. When he puts his head down on the table, O'Brien angrily warns him, "If you give up, they'll give up on you." His confidence is further challenged when his father visits and breaks down crying. Steve senses that his father is no longer sure of his son's innocence, and Steve feels ashamed and hopeless. He wonders what he did wrong but does not want to write in his journal about what happened because "I'd rather not have it in my mind," a line that casts a shadow of doubt on his innocence.

When his mother visits, Steve is deeply aware of her pain, and he also knows that she believes in his innocence. After she leaves, he examines his conscience: "And I knew she felt that I didn't do anything wrong. It was me who wasn't sure." This is a turning point in which Steve is no longer in denial. The movie script has allowed him to both disconnect and distance himself from assuming any responsibility, but now he admits that he wanted to be tough and impress the others; the section ends with a flashback in which King asks him to be a lookout, but the memory ends before Steve answers.

Steve subtly changes over the course of the novel, as he realizes that this experience is costing him the respect of his parents, friends, and little brother, Jerry. He expresses remorse and worries about what kind of example he is setting for Jerry. Steve understands the irony of his little brother not being allowed into the visitor's area because of his age: "if I wasn't locked up, I wouldn't be allowed to come into the visiting room."

The trial continues with more witnesses, including Richard "Bobo" Evans, "a big man, heavy, and ugly" who has been locked up for numerous crimes, including manslaughter. Now he is in prison for selling drugs. Bobo testifies that he and King committed the robbery and that, after Nesbitt was killed, he and King went to eat "fried chicken and wedgies," revealing their callous attitudes. He says that

Steve served as the lookout but then admits to O'Brien that Steve did not give any signal when Bobo came out of the store and that he and King did not meet up with Steve afterward or give him a share of the money.

O'Brien warns Steve not to act like a tough guy on the stand or else the jury will think that he is just like King. Steve testifies that he did not take part in the robbery and that he was not in the store. However, he wrote in his journal that he went into the store to buy mints, which means he must be lying under oath. Though the jury acquits Steve, the reader is left with the uneasy feeling that Steve is not completely innocent.

Steve never directly explains what happened that day, but he drops hints about his possible involvement. The readers know that Steve was in the store the day of the killing and that he had discussed his role with King. Furthermore, Steve's attorney and even his father, to a degree, seem to have some doubts about his innocence. Yet the reader also sympathizes with Steve and sees that he is a good student, a caring brother, and a sensitive young man. It is likely that Steve entered the store but did not actually give a signal; perhaps he had second thoughts, but at that point the robbery was already set in motion.

The novel dramatizes real-life temptations that alienated youth may face and attempts to give the reader an understanding of morals and self-worth. Even if Steve is innocent, his association with armed robbers and murderers incriminates him. He must take responsibility for his actions and his role in the crime. Five months after the trial is over, Steve spends much of his time making films about himself because "I want to know who I am." He cannot get out of his head the way O'Brien looked at him after he was acquitted and turned away from his hug: "What did she see?" No longer powerless, he is in the process of defining himself; he is fortunate to get another chance and can now make the right choices.

Major Themes

Myers wrote *Monster* in the late 1990s, a time when there was public outrage at the rise in juvenile crime and when many young black men were being tried as adults and sentenced to prison time. The novel portrays the pressure on young African-American males to prove their toughness, and it compassionately addresses how quickly children, by making the wrong choice, can lose their innocence in a single moment or by a sole rash act. By focusing on a 16-year-old African-American male, Myers also raises questions about the racism within the justice system and the moral issues of treating young people as adult criminals. A central theme in the novel is Steve's struggle to find himself and to distance himself from racial stereotypes. Other themes include questions about responsibility, individuality versus peer pressure, and harnessing creativity to express oneself.

Resisting Racial Stereotypes

Steve's lawyer informs him that the jury "believed you were guilty the moment they laid eyes on you. You're young, you're Black, and you're on trial." This charged line of dialogue reveals one of the main themes of the novel: In searching for his real self, Steve must resist the racist stereotyping that characterizes young black men as criminals. This stereotype is so common in society and popular culture that it has also greatly affected the justice system. Though he is supposed to be considered innocent until proven guilty, many of the jurors already assume he is guilty because of his race and age.

The prosecutor evokes the stereotype when she calls Steve a "monster." Steve feels like the word *monster* is "tattooed" on his forehead and seems to accept the prosecutor's description when he writes the word over and over on his paper, until O'Brien stops him. O'Brien recognizes that Steve will be lost if he accepts this negative stereotype as part of his true identity.

Other characters, including Bobo and King, seem to represent the very stereotype that Myers wants to negate. He uses them in order to serve as a contrast to Steve and to show what the future could hold for Steve if he continues to pursue a criminal route. Osvaldo, for instance, at the age of 14, is already on his way to becoming a Bobo; Myers also suggests that society is partly responsible by revealing how easily children without support or opportunities can fall into a life of crime.

Steve worries that by being in the detention center, he is essentially no different from the others. When he is mopping the floor, wearing the orange uniform, he realizes that the boys "must have all looked alike and I suddenly felt as if I couldn't breathe." In order to assert his true identity, Steve must define himself contrary to the stereotypes that are commonly held by society. The prison system nearly erodes his belief in himself, but in the end, he accepts responsibility and makes a genuine effort to regain his dignity and moral values.

Peer Pressure and Responsibility

The pressure to be tough is a major part of Steve's experience growing up, but Steve is not actually considered one of the tough guys, not like Osvaldo. Steve longs for a superhero's power, to be able to "kick butt." Before he went to jail, Steve wanted to impress men like Bobo and King and tried to emulate them. Because of his desire to be accepted, Steve fraternized with a questionable crowd, which led him to put his own future at risk.

In court, when King gives him a warning look, Steve suddenly understands that this kind of tough posturing will get him nowhere: "All the times I looked at him and wanted to be tough like him, and now I saw him sitting in handcuffs and trying to scare me." Steve wants to be "a good person," but by possibly participating in the robbery, he was responsible, in part, for the man's death. At first, he tries to distance himself and deny his role in the situation, but the truth is that he compromised his values for the sake of appearing "tough." By the end, he faces his own mistakes. Myers implies that, after Steve is acquitted, he will not succumb to peer pressure again but will devote his energy to improving himself and discovering his true identity.

ALICE WALKER

Biography

ALICE WALKER was born February 9, 1944, in Eatonton, Georgia, the eighth child of sharecroppers Willie Lee Walker and Minnie Tallulah. The oppression of the sharecropping system and the racism of the South would significantly influence Walker's early years and subsequently her writing. When she was eight, she became blind in one eye after one of her brothers accidentally shot her with a BB gun. Feeling ashamed of the disfigurement, she isolated herself from other children and spent her time reading and writing.

After graduating as valedictorian of her class, in 1961 Walker went to Spelman College in Atlanta on full scholarship and later transferred to Sarah Lawrence College in Bronxville, New York, graduating in 1965. She became active in the civil rights movement and returned to the South, where she became involved with voter-registration drives, campaigns for welfare rights, and children's programs in Mississippi. In 1967, Walker married Mel Leventhal, a civil-rights lawyer. As the first legally married interracial couple in Mississippi, they faced harassment and threats. The couple moved back to New York and had a daughter, Rebecca, in 1969. They divorced eight years later.

Walker wrote her first book of poetry, *Once*, while she was still a senior at Sarah Lawrence. She published her first novel, *The Third Life of Grange Copeland*, in 1970, followed by a short story collection *In Love and Trouble* (1973), which contained her widely anthologized short story "Everyday Use." Walker's seminal essay "The Search for Zora Neale Hurston," published in *Ms.* magazine in 1974, was largely responsible for the renewal of interest in the work of the African-American writer Zora Neale Hurston. Walker searched for and discovered Hurston's unmarked grave, placing a monument there to honor the life of the once-forgotten author. Walker taught at various colleges throughout the 1970s and also worked as an editor for *Ms.* magazine. She moved to San Francisco in 1978 and continues to live in California.

In 1982, Walker published her best-known and most widely praised work, *The Color Purple*, which concerns a young black woman struggling to survive in a racist and male-dominated culture. The novel became a best-seller and received the National Book Award and the Pulitzer Prize for fiction in 1983—Walker was the first African-American woman to win the prestigious prize. The novel also touched off controversy among critics and some black scholars who accused Walker of negatively portraying black men as either unintelligent or abusive and violent. The novel was adapted into a critically acclaimed movie directed by Steven Spielberg and starring Whoopi Goldberg and Oprah Winfrey. It was nominated for 11 Academy Awards and was adapted into a successful 2005 Broadway musical.

A leading voice among black American women writers, Alice Walker has produced a varied and prolific body of work, including poetry, novels, short stories, essays, and criticism. Other works of fiction include *Meridian* (1976), about activist workers in the South during the civil rights movement; *You Can't Keep a Good Woman Down: Stories* (1982); *The Temple of My Familiar* (1989); and *Now Is the Time to Open Your Heart* (2005).

Walker has described herself as a *womanist*, her term for a black feminist, which she defines in the introduction to her collection of essays, *In Search of Our Mothers' Gardens: Womanist Prose* (1984). Her writing focuses on the struggles, survival, and liberation of black women living in a racist and sexist society; she explores the problems that black women face in both the United States and Africa. *Possessing the Secret of Joy* (1992), for example, which features several characters from *The Color Purple*, focuses on the consequences of Tashi's decision to undergo a clitoridectomy or surgical removal of the clitoris. Walker's nonfiction work *Warrior Marks* (1996) also concerns female genital mutilation in Africa. Other themes she explores in her work include the oppression of poverty, the preservation of black culture, and the importance of ancestral lineage. All of Walker's work revolves around women, their spirituality, creativity, strength, and endurance. The women in her books summon these qualities to triumph over oppression and hardship.

"Everyday Use"
Plot and Analysis

Walker's most widely read short story focuses on a mother and her daughters and their relationship to and understanding of their African-American heritage. The story takes place around the late 1960s or early 1970s in a rural area somewhere in the Deep South in a single afternoon. The protagonist, Mama (Mrs. Johnson), is also the story's narrator.

Mama and her daughter Maggie, who share a small, three-room house, are awaiting the arrival of Dee, Maggie's sister. In preparation, they have neatly swept the dirt yard so that it resembles "an extended living room." The atmosphere is serene and quiet, yet there is an undercurrent of tension as they wait for Dee. Mama knows that Maggie will be nervous and will look at her sister "with a mixture of envy and awe."

Mama wishes that she and Dee could happily reunite and mend their differences like the people on television. In the fantasy, Mama imagines herself to be "the way my daughter would want me to be": light skinned, witty, and about 100 pounds lighter. Dee is ashamed of the reality: Mama is a "large, big-bone woman with rough, man-working hands." She is not a witty conversationalist but a hard worker who can "kill and clean a hog as mercilessly as a man." Though Mama is strong, she also knows she would never be as fearless as Dee to look "a strange white man in the eye."

A dozen years ago, Dee watched happily as their old house burned down. For her, its demise symbolized her freedom. Maggie was burned in the fire and is ashamed of the scars that resulted, which suggest the legacy of slavery, the violence and brutality that black Americans like her had suffered. Mama raised money with a local church to send Dee away to school, but Maggie, seen as "not bright," stayed with her mother. Maggie represents the poor, uneducated, oppressed black woman. She shuffles when she walks, barely speaks, and hides her face. She will marry a farmboy, "who has mossy teeth in an earnest face."

The opposite of her sister, Dee possesses beauty, style, and flair. She arrives with a companion, a black Muslim man whose name Mama cannot pronounce. Dee greets her mother and sister with an African phrase and, like a tourist, takes their picture, "making sure the house is included." Dee is dressed in African costume, "a dress so loud it hurts my eyes": everything about Dee is loud, contrasted to Maggie, who shirks into corners. During the time in which the story is set, the Back to Africa movement was becoming more popular in the United States. The movement advocated the discovery and reclaiming of African ancestry, instead of the focus being traditionally placed on the history of slavery and injustice. Walker is not denouncing the movement, but she shows that for Dee and her companion, the movement is a fad, and they do not truly grasp their African roots. For example, Mama contrasts Dee's partner, Hakim-a-barber, who professes the movement's ideology in an unearnest, almost unbelievable way, with the hardworking, admirable Muslim farmers who live nearby.

Dee has renamed herself Wangero, an African name she has adopted. Though she knows that she was named after her aunt, Big Dee, she does not know how far the name went back, revealing her ignorance of her own heritage and legacy. Mama believes that she could trace the name back to before the Civil War, but Dee insists she was named after her oppressors. Dee patronizingly views her mother and sister's lives as quaint: "Everything delighted her." They are living in the past, and since Dee/Wangero no longer feels any connection to such old-fashioned ways, she views their lives in a patronizing manner. She claims the butter churn, for instance, not for its practical aspects but in order to use the top as a centerpiece. Dee does not know its history, but Maggie does. In relating its origin, Maggie speaks for the first time: "'Aunt Dee's first husband whittled the dash,' said Maggie so low you almost couldn't hear her. 'His name was Henry, but they called him Stash.'"

Dee also now wants to take two quilts, though at one point her mother had offered them to her and she refused them because "they were old-fashioned, out of style." For Mama, the quilts hold great significance, representing the members of the family. When Mama resists Dee's request, saying she already promised the quilts to Maggie for her dowry, Dee angrily lashes out that Maggie will not appreciate them. For Maggie, the quilts represent a memory of her grandmother; nonetheless, looking like she is "used to never winning anything," Maggie concedes ownership and says her sister can have them.

Mama looks "hard" at Maggie and for the first time sees beyond her daughter's "dopey, hangdog look." Maggie, who learned to quilt from her grandmother, represents a connection to the ancestors. In Maggie's scarred hands, Mama sees their heritage, and she wants Maggie to be proud. For the first time, Mama says no to Dee. She snags the quilts out of Dee's hands and gives them to Maggie.

Dee angrily accuses her mother of not understanding her "heritage." As she tells them goodbye, she puts on sunglasses that hide her face, a symbol of Dee's inability to see her own heritage clearly. In contrast, Maggie smiles "a real smile, not scared." For the first time, Dee's visit does not make Maggie or her mother feel bad about their lives; instead, they see Dee as the foolish one. After she leaves, Mama and Maggie relax in the yard, using snuff and resuming the comforting rituals that characterize their lives.

Major Themes

Walker's dedication of "Everyday Use" to "your grandmamma," is relevant: This is a story that celebrates African-American heritage, female ancestors, and the strength of black women. Walker gives a voice to the uneducated, poor black woman, allowing her to speak and be heard. The story also explores themes of Africanism (the study of African culture), tensions between the generations, the meaning of tradition, and the idea of art versus "everyday use."

The Importance of Heritage

Irony enters the story when Dee accuses her mother of not understanding her heritage, when it is she who has willfully disconnected herself from her family and cultural background. Dee tries to claim her African roots, despite making no attempt to understand her ancestors and the past of her people. The items around the house hold no real meaning for her. She does not know the objects' histories, as her sister does, and even more significantly, she does not even know the origin of her own name. The quilts that she wants to hang on the walls link her to previous generations and to the African-American past of slavery, oppression, and violent racism, but she views them as decoration, adornments as opposed to heirlooms.

Dee's lack of knowledge about her family reveals that her feelings about her heritage are superficial and shallow. It is Maggie, the uneducated one, who values the family heritage. When Mama gives Maggie the quilts, Maggie is thrilled because the connection to her women ancestors and her identity is reaffirmed. The short story is a slice of rural, black everyday life, in which a significant change occurs: Now Mama and Dee fully claim and feel proud of their heritage.

Art Versus "Everyday Use"

For Dee, the objects in her mother's house are relics of the past, not a part of her real and actual life. She wants to display the butter churn as an artwork or mere decorative element and to hang the quilts on the wall to be admired like paintings in a museum. Quilting was a tradition, a ritual among poor southern black women who patched together scraps to create quilts of stunning beauty. Critic Elaine Showalter observes in her essay "Piecing and Writing": "In contemporary writing, the quilt stands for a vanished past experience to which we have a troubled and ambivalent cultural relationship" (228). Though the quilts are a reminder of slavery, they are also powerful symbols of resistance and female bonding. The quilts in the Johnson family remind Mama and Maggie of the family history: Grandma Dee, Big Dee, and Mama made the quilts from scraps of her grandmother's dresses and a piece of the uniform worn by the great-grandfather who served in the Union Army in the Civil War.

Maggie learned this tradition—how to take scraps and turn them into something creative and useful—from her female ancestors. When Dee, whose desire to hang the quilts as art denies their history and purpose, exclaims that Maggie would "probably be backward enough to put them to everyday use," Mama explains that the quilts are meant to be used. If they wear out, then Maggie "can always make some more." In the end, Mama realizes that she should not have hidden the quilts in a trunk, and she places them in Maggie's hands, passing on tradition and the family legacy in doing so. Quilting is an art, but the art will not die as long as there are people like Maggie to carry on the practice.

The Color Purple
Summary and Analysis

The Color Purple follows the struggles and eventual triumph of Celie, a poor, abused, uneducated African-American woman. The novel is epistolary (told through a series of diary entries and letters) and takes place in rural Georgia, beginning in the early 1900s and ending in the mid-1940s.

Celie writes private letters to God that resemble a diary, documenting the abuse she suffers and revealing her lack of self-esteem. The dialect and first-person voice create an intimacy and authenticity, allowing us to enter Celie's mind and witness her development. As a poor African-American woman and a victim of domestic abuse, Celie is almost completely voiceless. The letters provide a way for her to break the silence forced on her.

At 14, Celie is repeatedly beaten and raped by her father, Alphonso. After he impregnates her twice, he steals the babies from her, presumably killing the

The white prison warden is Squeak's uncle, and Albert and the others convince her to trick the warden into releasing Sofia by using subtle wordplay. Though Sofia is released from prison to work as a maid for the mayor's family, Squeak pays severely when the warden brutally rapes her. Squeak asserts her identity by instructing Harpo to call her by her real name, and from that moment on, Squeak literally finds her voice and begins singing. Critic Lauren Berlant attests, "Having exposed herself to sexual, racial, and political abuse in the name of communal solidarity, Squeak assumes the right to her given name, Mary Agnes. She also earns the right to 'sing'" (2002). The theme of a woman discovering her voice is important in the novel. Celie, Shug, Nettie, Squeak, and Sofia all use their voices in different ways to resist oppression.

When Shug returns, she is married to Grady, upsetting both Albert and Celie, who are each in love with her. Despite Shug's new husband, Shug and Celie grow closer. Celie tells Shug that her father raped her, the first time she has ever spoken about it. No longer numb, she cries. The intimacy between the women deepens, and they become lovers. Celie not only discovers her own voice and strength of character, but she also reclaims her body and sexuality. One night, Shug asks about Nettie. Celie assumes her sister is dead, since she has not received any letters. But Shug has noticed Albert hiding letters and manages to get her hands on one: It is from Nettie, one of dozens of such letters they find hidden in Albert's trunk.

Nettie is now given the opportunity to add her voice to the narrative, and the letters become a second story within the novel. Nettie befriends a missionary couple, Samuel and Corrine, and their adopted children, Olivia and Adam, and travels with them to Africa, where they stay in the Olinka village. Through Nettie's letters, Walker exposes the tensions between black Americans and native Africans, the destruction of European imperialism, and the intense sexism that marked African life.

When Corrine becomes ill with a fever, she becomes upset because she believes that the children are Samuel and Nettie's, since they resemble Nettie. Nettie learns the story of how they adopted Olivia and Adam, and she realizes that they are Celie's biological children. She also learns that Alphonso is actually their stepfather; their real father was a store owner who was lynched by white men who resented his success. After Corrine learns the real story of her children, she finally accepts the explanation as the truth and dies. Samuel and Nettie realize they are deeply in love and eventually marry. Soon, they plan to return to the United States.

Celie is so angry that Albert had hidden the letters that she wants to kill him. Angry with God, she now addresses her letters to Nettie and says of God: "If he ever listened to poor colored women the world would be a different place, I can tell you." Shug surprises Celie by telling her that she believes in God; however, instead of the typical white male God, Shug sees God as genderless, present in the flowers and the sky and "the color purple in a field." Shug helps Celie to see that there are different ways of living and thinking, helping Celie move closer to her own liberation and independence. The conversation challenges Celie's spirituality, and she begins to be more aware of the beauty around her: "Now that my eyes opening, I feels like a fool."

Celie's letters reveal her emotional and spiritual growth. In the beginning, she only reported events and did not analyze her emotions, but now she makes astute observations, offers opinions, and analyzes and interprets her feelings.

In a climactic scene, when everyone is gathered at the dinner table, Celie confronts Albert about hiding Nettie's letters. It is the first time she speaks out against him: "You a lowdown dog is what's wrong." For Celie, this is a major turning point; with a new sense of power, she expresses her growing resentment and curses Albert for the years of abuse: "You made my life a hell on earth."

Everyone at the table is shocked, especially Sofia, who, after nearly 12 years of servitude, has lost her rebellious spirit: "Sofia so surprise to hear me speak up she ain't chewed for ten minutes." Sofia spent nearly 12 years in servitude to the mayor's family, and now, returned to her own, she feels lost. The older children have left, and the younger ones do not recognize her; the mayor's family also continues to bother her with their troubles, not caring that she has her own family and personal concerns.

Celie's outburst causes a ripple effect among the women. Sofia's fiery spirit and passion are rekindled, and she looks at Harpo and "laugh[s] in his face." Mary Agnes announces that she is going to become a singer. Furious, Albert tries to define Celie: "You black, you pore, you ugly, you a woman . . . you nothing at all," expressing the major theme of the novel. As the least empowered in American society, how can an impoverished black woman succeed? Celie responds that all of that may be true, "But I'm here," asserting the basic and essential fact of her existence.

Shug, Grady, Mary Agnes, and Celie leave for Memphis where Shug lives in a large pink house, decorated with elephants and turtles. Celie, given her own room, expresses her creativity for the first time by sewing pants for her, Shug, and Squeak. Shug encourages Celie to take the sewing one step further by starting her own business. After her stepfather dies, Celie inherits the land and house and decides to move back, relocating her pants business. An important part of Celie's empowerment is her newfound economic independence. She has an income, business, home, friends, and a lover. The critic bell hooks, however, argues that now Celie has everything her oppressors once had and questions whether there has been any radical change: "Walker creates fiction wherein an oppressed black woman can experience self-recovery without . . . collective political effort; without radical change in society," calling it a "fantasy of every desire fulfilled" (295). But a part of this fantasy dissolves when Shug leaves her for a young man; Celie is heartbroken.

In Africa, Nettie and Samuel are meanwhile preparing to return to the United States. Before they leave, Adam marries an African girl, Tashi, who undergoes the ritual of female circumcision and facial scarring. To show solidarity, Adam undergoes the same ritualistic facial scarring. Celie is expecting their arrival but then receives a telegram from the U.S. government informing her that the ship transporting Nettie and her family had been bombed by the Germans.

Though sadness overwhelms the novel, there is also redemption. Celie no longer feels hatred or anger toward Albert, and she feels connected to him because he is the only one who can understand her heartache in losing Shug. Albert, also, is a changed man—he is sorry for the way he treated Celie and now shows her respect. When he asks her if she wants to be married again and asks about her sexual attractions, she tells him that she feels no desire for men. They spend much of their time together: "Here us is, I thought, two old fools left over from love, keeping each other company under the stars." In the end, she no longer thinks of him as Mr. _____, but as Albert, symbolizing a shift in her perception of herself: Now they are on equal ground.

Meanwhile, Sofia and Harpo remarry, and Sofia asserts her independence by telling Eleanor Jane, the mayor's daughter, that while she appreciates the kindness she showed her, that does not mean that she has to love Eleanor Jane's baby. Essentially, Sophia is saying that she has her own family and life, which were taken away from her and deeply compromised by Eleanor Jane's parents. The conversation provokes Eleanor Jane to ask her mother why Sofia came to work for them in the first place, and the mayor's daughter is upset when she hears the truth. In a reversal of social roles, Eleanor Jane helps take care of Henrietta, Sofia's daughter, while Sofia works in Celie's store.

Celie recovers from her separation from Shug and opens her heart: "Who am I to tell her who to love?" Celie feels confident that Shug will return and also continues to hope that one day she will see Nettie. After Shug breaks up with her younger boyfriend, she returns to Celie. But the family reunion is not complete until the day that Nettie, Samuel, and the children arrive. The family, related both by blood and by mutual choice, finally comes together, like a quilt, and Celie, who has grown into an emotionally, financially, and spiritually independent woman, feels a youthful joy denied her until now.

Major Themes

The Color Purple is a "womanist" novel, exposing and denouncing patriarchy and depicting a community of women freeing themselves from their oppressors. Walker also examines relationships between African Americans and native Africans and the destructive effects of imperialism, racism, and classism. The novel also raises questions about sexuality, spirituality, and economic freedom. By focusing on Celie's struggles and triumphs, Walker reveals the power of female community and the liberation in breaking down oppressive gender roles.

Womanist Community

The most dominant theme in the novel concerns how a strong community of black women leads to solidarity, liberation, and independence. There are many strong female relationships portrayed in the novel, from sisters and mothers to friends and lovers. The relationships Celie establishes with the other women bolster her strength and contribute to her emerging as a fully realized individual.

Early in the narrative, Celie watches how Sofia, the first strong female she encounters, stands up to her husband. Sofia explains that she comes from a family of five close sisters who bonded together to fight off their brothers; the deep ties among women allowed them to combat sexism and abuse. Celie also observes how the timid Squeak finally asserts her own identity and is no longer mouselike. With the help of Shug, who moves freely through life, Celie turns into a woman who is confident and strong. Walker explores how family is not necessarily defined by DNA or blood relations but by supportive relationships. For example, after Nettie's letters suddenly reveal new information about Celie's family history, she tries but fails to find her mother's grave. Shug reassures her: "Us each other's peoples now."

With the support of Shug, Sophie, and Squeak, Celie finally feels strong enough to leave Albert. The community of women and Celie's own growing independence give her the self-esteem needed to resist Albert's definition of her as "nothing." By the end of the novel, she is able to forgive Albert and develop a close friendship with him. However, her closest relationships are with women, as witnessed when Nettie finally returns. Though they have not seen each other for many years, their sisterly love runs deep and has kept them bonded nonetheless: "Us totter toward one nother like us use to do when us was babies. Then us feel so weak when us touch, us knock each other down. But what us care? Us sit and lay there on the porch inside each other's arms."

Breaking Down Gender Roles

To resist or weaken the male-dominated society the novel's women inhabit, gender roles must be changed or broken down. Walker reveals many instances in the novel that call gender roles into question. Harpo, for example, prefers housekeeping to yardwork, whereas Sofia would rather be chopping wood or out in the fields, occupied with what was traditionally identified as "men's work." Harpo, initially pressured to "be a man," insists on his superiority by attempting but failing to beat Sofia into submission. By the end of the novel, he has changed and finally accepts Sofia on her own terms.

Traditionally, men were looked to as the earners, the providers of survival and sustenance. But Shug is independently successful and wealthy, and she convinces Celie to turn her love of sewing pants into a business, helping her achieve financial freedom. It is significant that she sews pants, traditionally men's clothing, for women; the pants symbolize Celie's independence and the shedding of her role as submissive wife. Celie becomes self-sufficient, taking a traditionally domestic chore for women and turning it into a profitable business.

Similarly, Shug and Squeak use their creative talents for singing as a way to earn a living and achieve independence. Celie teaches Albert to sew, not a traditionally male activity, and they sit on the porch, sewing, talking, and smoking pipes. These seemingly small actions contribute to breaking down boundaries of gender roles and cracking apart the male-controlled system, allowing freedom and independence to take its place.

AUGUST WILSON

Biography

AUGUST WILSON was born Frederick August Kittel on April 27, 1945, in the Hill District of Pittsburgh, Pennsylvania, the fourth of six children. His father was a German immigrant baker, who spent very little time with his family, and his mother, Daisy Wilson, was an African-American cleaning woman. Wilson and his siblings were raised by his mother in a two-room apartment in a neighborhood inhabited predominantly by African Americans and Jewish and Italian immigrants. In the late 1950s, his mother married David Bedford, and the family moved to a predominantly white working-class neighborhood, Hazelwood, where they encountered intense racial hostility. Wilson, the only African-American student at his high school, faced daily racist encounters; he dropped out at 15, after a teacher accused him of plagiarizing a research paper.

Wilson educated himself at the Carnegie Library, reading many black writers including Ralph Ellison, Richard Wright, and Langston Hughes. He enlisted in the U.S. Army in 1962 and left after one year, working a series of odd jobs including porter, short-order cook, gardener, and dishwasher. After his father's death in 1965, he changed his name to August Wilson to honor his mother. That same year he bought his first typewriter.

During the 1960s, Wilson wrote poetry and was involved in the Black Power movement. He co-founded the Black Horizon Theater in the Hill District of Pittsburgh, and his first play, *Recycling*, was performed for audiences in small theaters and public-housing community centers. In the late 1970s, Wilson moved to Saint Paul, Minnesota, where he wrote educational scripts for the Science Museum of Minnesota and won a fellowship at the Minneapolis Playwrights Center. Wilson's breakthrough came with *Ma Rainey's Black Bottom*, directed by Lloyd Richards in 1983, at the O'Neill Workshop in Waterford,

Connecticut. Richards would direct six of Wilson's plays, all of which premiered at the Yale Repertory Theater.

In 1990, Wilson moved to Washington State to work with Seattle Repertory Theatre, the only theater in the country to produce all of his works. Over the span of his career, Wilson won two Pulitzer Prizes, seven New York Drama Critics' Circle Awards, and earned many fellowships and honorary degrees. On August 26, 2005, he told the *Pittsburgh Post-Gazette* that he had been diagnosed with liver cancer and had three to five months to live. He died on October 2, 2005, in Seattle and was survived by his third wife, costume designer Constanza Romero, and his two daughters.

Wilson's literary legacy is a group of 10 plays called the Pittsburgh Cycle, which include his best-known works: *Ma Rainey's Black Bottom* (1984), *Fences* (1987), *Joe Turner's Come and Gone* (1988), *The Piano Lesson* (1990), and *Two Trains Running* (1992). Nine of the 10 plays that make up the Pittsburgh Cycle are set in Pittsburgh's Hill District, an African-American neighborhood that served as Wilson's mythical literary setting, similar to William Faulkner's Yoknapatawpha County.

Wilson's writing was inspired by what he called the "4 B's": the blues, which allows characters to communicate otherwise unspeakable tragedies and triumphs; Amiri Bakara, fellow playwright, poet, and leading figure in the Black Arts movement; metaphysical author Jorge Luis Borges; and African-American painter Romare Bearden, whose collages and patchwork paintings have been likened to a visual expression of the blues. Wilson saw theater as a way to raise awareness about black life in the United States and committed himself to writing the cycle of 10 plays that would rewrite the history of each decade of the twentieth century.

One major theme in Wilson's plays is the tension between African Americans who want to hold onto their African heritage and family legacy and those who want to break away from its influence and demands. Wilson also tends to focus on African-American male characters, evoking themes that arise from father-son relationships. His plays promote the importance of black history and yet do not rely on historical accuracy as much as they do artistic imagination. Wilson's main themes relate to racial injustice and alienation, and he transforms select moments in American history as opportunities for the African-American community to examine and define itself and for individuals to choose their own futures.

Fences
Summary and Analysis

Divided into two acts, *Fences* examines an African-American family trying to obtain their dreams in a postwar pre–civil rights America that is rife with racial discrimination. Despite this prevailing condition, the era also teeters on the brink of change, with opportunities for African Americans slowly increasing. The protagonist, 53-year-old Troy Maxson, is dynamic, charming, and larger than life; his mix of strengths and flaws makes him powerful but destructive. He lives with his wife, Rose, and their son, Cory, in an "ancient two-story brick house" in a rundown section of Pittsburgh, with a small dirt yard that is only partially fenced. The shabby setting symbolizes Troy's lost or compromised dreams.

The play begins on a Friday night. It is payday, and Troy and Jim Bono, garbage collectors, are engaged in their weekly ritual of talking and drinking. The opening dialogue both foreshadows the plot of the play and reveals their close friendship. Bono looks up to Troy for his honesty and strength. That Troy recently asked their boss why there are no black truck drivers in the company is an example of his courage as well as a demonstration of his resentment about racist policies.

When Bono implies that Troy is having an affair with "that Alberta girl," Troy becomes defensive, proclaiming his love for Rose. He displays his male bravado when Rose comes onto the porch. Rose, 10 years younger than Troy and extremely devoted to him, lives under his looming shadow. She sets the play's central conflict into motion when she informs Troy that a college football recruiter is interested in Cory.

Cory excels at football the way Troy used to excel at baseball. Although Troy played for the Negro Leagues, he did not get a chance to play in the Major Leagues because of its segregation policy; by the time the league began accepting black players, Troy was too old to play. Fixated on this opportunity that he was deprived of, Troy refuses to listen when Rose and Bono try to tell him that things are changing. He convinces himself that the discrimination in sports will only likewise disappoint his son and "ain't gonna get him nowhere."

Troy is a boastful, confident, and charismatic storyteller; one of his favorite stories is about his victory over death. Throughout the play, Troy's anecdotes and monologues entertain those around him while also serving as a defense or as a way to justify his own mistakes. Both Rose and Bono endure Troy's exaggerations, though they recognize the distortion and altered facts. The stories are harmless, yet they reveal how Troy has trouble accepting or recognizing reality, and they foreshadow the more damaging lies he will conjure.

An unemployed, would-be jazz musician, Lyons, Troy's 34-year-old son from a previous marriage, stops by to his see his father only when he needs money. The opposite of Troy, Lyons is irresponsible and feels no sense of duty to work. Though Troy does not approve of his son's lifestyle, Troy feels guilty that he was not around for Lyons's childhood because he was in prison; he makes up for his absence by loaning his son money. As they go through their weekly ritual, Troy amicably humiliates and scolds Lyons but loans him the money in a familiar ceremony that makes it clear to everyone that he is the sole provider.

Scene 2 begins with Troy criticizing Rose for playing the lottery. Troy takes pride in his financial responsibility; ironically, he engages in other kinds of risky behaviors that threaten to harm or destroy his family. Troy's brother, Gabriel, makes his first appearance. Suffering a major head injury sustained in World War II, Gabriel carries an old trumpet with him and believes that he is the Archangel Gabriel. Suggesting the figure of the wise fool, he is nonsensical yet also dispenses wisdom. Gabriel used to live with Rose and Troy but now he lives with the neighbor Miss Pearl, paying his rent with the government subsidy that used to go to Troy. Gabriel worries that Troy is angry with him now that the money goes to him, the rightful recipient. Without his brother's subsidy, Troy would not have been able to buy a home for his family, something he feels ashamed and bitter about. Troy recognizes the irony in his brother's situation: He served for a country that denies him equal rights.

Cory helps Troy work on the fence in scene 3. When Cory asks if they can get a television, Troy says any extra money will be used to tar the roof; however, he offers to pay for half of the television if Cory can come up with the rest. Though he compromises on the new purchase, when it comes to sports, Troy is antagonistic and stubborn. He complains about the racism that dominates sports, and when Cory, who views society as moving into a more accepting place, offers examples of successful African-American players, Troy ignores him.

Though Cory earns good grades, works at a grocery store, and is responsible, Troy only focuses on the football; he tells Cory he wants him to quit. He thinks his son would have more of a future if he learned a trade. Hurt, Cory asks, "How come you ain't never liked me?" Instead of showing his son affection, Troy replies by defining his role as a father in terms of his duties.

Two weeks later, in scene 4, which parallels the opening scene, Troy and Bono are drinking on a Friday after work. Both men are happy because Troy has been promoted: Despite being illiterate and without a driver's license, he will be the first black driver for the company. The men are thrilled that Troy challenged racist practices and succeeded—a rarity in their lives. For a fleeting moment, a feeling of possibility prevails. Lyons shows up to pay his father back, and Gabriel comes by to say he's been "chasing hellhounds."

Troy and Bono discuss their fathers, who were products of Reconstruction. After slavery was abolished, the Reconstruction era failed to help dislocated and economically depressed African Americans enter mainstream society. Bono's father, with the "walking blues," abandoned the family, but Troy's father, a struggling sharecropper, stayed to raise 11 children. However, he viewed them as nothing more than field hands. Troy learned his strong work ethic from his father but suffered under his cruelty. Troy's own path to manhood resulted from a traumatic break with his father, after his father tried to rape Troy's girlfriend. Troy stood up to his father, and after his father beat him badly, Troy "bec[a]me a man" and left home. However, he soon discovered that there were few opportunities in the North and fell into a life of crime, which ended when he was sentenced to 15 years for manslaughter. In prison, he met Bono and learned to play baseball.

Troy has tried to live his life differently from his father, but he still confuses love with duty. The most obvious example of this is his failing relationship with Cory, who comes home enraged that his father told the coach that he can no longer play football. He believes that his father is making him pay for his own failed dreams: "You just scared I'm gonna be better than you, that's all."

In act 2, scene 1, Troy bails Gabriel out of jail; whenever the children in town provoke Gabriel, he is locked up and Troy must pay $50 for his release. Later, Troy, Bono, and Cory work on the fence. As the dominant symbol in the play, the fence holds multiple meanings. For Troy, it is a sign of ownership and control. The fence also symbolizes Troy's alienation, a representation of the fences he builds between him and others. Rose is actually the one who wants the fence built, but only Bono understands her reason: "to keep people in" and hold her family together.

After Cory leaves, Troy admits to Bono that he is having an affair, and Bono wants him to do the right thing by Rose. Troy finally tells Rose the truth: "I'm gonna be somebody's daddy." The audience is surprised by this information and realizes how deeply Troy has been living in denial of his own actions. Troy tries to justify his affair, explaining that being with Alberta gives him a sense of freedom, allowing him "to steal second." Throughout the play, Troy flavors his speech with baseball imagery, viewing baseball as a metaphor for life.

Shocked and devastated, Rose finds her voice: "We're not talking about baseball!" Rose, who has spent 18 years at Troy's side, is repaid with his betrayal. Troy feels entitled to the affair, viewing it as payback for the injustices he has faced. He shows no remorse and does not apologize. When Rose tells him that he only takes and does not give, he reacts by violently grabbing her. Cory knocks his father to the ground, and everyone is stunned.

Act 2, scene 2 revisits the family six months later. Rose now rarely speaks to her husband except to ask if he is coming home after work, and Troy admits that he will be at the hospital because Alberta is delivering the baby. Then Rose informs him that Gabriel has been committed to the asylum because Troy signed documents authorizing the move and granting him half of Gabriel's assets. Troy, who cannot read, feels ashamed; again, he has destroyed or damaged the dreams of someone he loves.

The phone rings, and Rose delivers the tragic news: Alberta died during childbirth. Troy pushes down "a quiet rage that threatens to consume him" and lashes out at death. In a last attempt to assert control, he will build the fence to keep death out: "You stay over there until you're ready for me."

Act 2, scene 3 begins three days later, when Troy arrives at the house, carrying his baby. He sits on the porch and sings a blues song about a man begging a train engineer to let him ride for free; the lyrics reveal his dire situation, his sense of entrapment, lack of options, and inability to escape his present situation. When he finally appeals to Rose, she lets him in and agrees to take care of the baby; but, she warns him, "you a womanless man."

Two months later, in act 2, scene 4, an independent Rose is preparing for a church bake sale. She has transferred her devotion from Troy to the church. Lyons, stuck in the same cycle, arrives to pay his father back for a loan, while Cory, graduated from high school, is looking for a job.

On payday, Troy sits on the porch and drinks alone, singing a blues song. Bono stops by for the first time since Troy admitted the affair; now that Troy is a truck driver, he and Bono see very little of each other. Troy wants Bono to stay and drink like old times, but now Bono plays dominoes on Fridays with other men from work. This scene sharply contrasts with the opening scene. Bono used to look up to Troy, but now, after feeling let down by his friend, he, like Rose, asserts his independence and seeks out other people or sources of comfort.

When Cory walks by, Troy physically blocks his progress. Troy demands his respect, but Cory says: "You don't count around here no more." Their escalating tension culminates in a violent confrontation, which ends when Troy stands over his son with a bat, holding himself back from delivering the final blow. He kicks Cory out, telling him that his possessions "will be on the other side of that fence." The fence symbolizes how Troy is separated from others, locked in his own loneliness. Troy has lost his best friend, his wife, and his son and yet still tries to maintain his dignity.

Act 2, scene 5 takes place eight years later, in 1965, on the morning of Troy's funeral. Finally defeated by death, Troy died while he was at the tree, swinging his bat. This final scene shows the family going on without Troy. Seven-year-old Raynell plays in the dirt of her new garden, waiting for the seeds to grow. Lyons is released from the workhouse where he is doing time for cashing other people's checks. Cory is also home for the first time in almost eight years. He is wearing a Marine corporal's uniform and is engaged.

Cory does not want to go to the funeral because he wants to escape from his father's "shadow." Rose admits that Troy made many mistakes. She realizes now that she should have made him leave "some room for me." But Rose points out that Cory possesses his father's fighting spirit, redeeming the father figure for Cory and convincing him to tear down the fences between father and son.

Raynell feels no negative feelings toward her father. As the new generation, she represents the change taking place not only in the house but in the country. In the years since Cory left, the civil rights movement has gained force and power. The generations are brought together as Cory and Raynell sing the song their father used to sing about Blue the dog. The use of the blues as a way of reconciling the past is a common motif in Wilson's work. Finally, Cory can forgive his father, realizing that Troy did what he could with what he had learned in life.

Released from the hospital for the funeral, Gabriel plays his trumpet. When no sound comes out, he begins to dance and howl in a ritual that conveys his and the family's connection to their African ancestry. This ritual allows the family to reconcile the past and look beyond the fence to the future.

Major Themes

Fences portrays the failures of the post–World War II American Dream for many African Americans and their hope for change. Troy Maxson struggles as a husband, father, and black man in racist America. His past and the many obstacles he faces have shaped his ideas about how to survive. To the disappointment of his son and wife, Troy refuses to see that progress is slowly being made. Themes also include the construction of black masculinity, the disillusion of father-son relationships, and how relationships fail when individuals build walls between one another or cling to illusions.

Fatherhood

One of the major themes in *Fences* is the complicated experience of fatherhood and the turbulent relationships between fathers and sons. Troy Maxson defies racist stereotypes of the absent black father. He lives with his family, works a full-time job, and does not shirk from responsibility. He loans money to Lyons, takes care of his brother, and when he is at his lowest point, he takes responsibility for Raynell. However, while it is true that Troy never actually deserts his family, he pushes them away. He measures his success as a father and husband by what he provides, "I give you my sweat and my blood"; but what they really want are his affection and love.

One of the main focuses of the play is the disintegration of the relationship between Troy and Cory. Though he tries to protect Cory from life's disappointments, Troy only ends up hurting him. He asserts control over Cory's quest for independence, and this power dynamic alienates the son from the father. To secure his own future, Cory must confront his father and then leave him, as Troy did with his own father, a man who was beaten down by oppression. After Troy made his break with his father, he thought he would find success and independence. Instead, like his father, he encountered a society that left black men too often feeling powerless and alienated.

The legacy of the father culminates in the climactic scene where Troy and Cory fight. Though Troy has tried to define himself in contrast to his father, here he mirrors him, pushing his own son away, stopping himself, however, from delivering the final blow. By evoking his own father's legacy, Troy builds fences between himself and those who love him.

Illusions of the American Dream

Fences gives voice to those African Americans who were tempted by the lure of the American Dream yet did not have access to the freedoms and equality needed to bring about the success and self-improvement the dream implies. This theme echoes the subject of Lorraine Hansberry's *A Raisin in the Sun*, which examines the economic and social effects of racism on a family that strives to attain the myth.

Similarly, Troy, a black man of lower economic status, is alienated from the dominant culture, representing the gap between the American Dream and the African Americans who sought to improve their economic standing. Though Troy works full time, he will never earn enough to obtain the 1950s American ideal. He feels guilty and ashamed that he has had to rely on Gabriel's injury in order to get "a roof over my head." Furthermore, Troy is forced to give up his dream of playing in the Major Leagues: "I just wasn't the right color." Angry and bitter, he feels that now it is too late to take advantage of the social changes stirring around him. Caught between being responsible and being free to pursue his dreams, Troy risks his marriage by having an affair, using it as a way to distract his powerful sense of denied opportunities.

Cory represents the new wave of optimism and hope the next generation possessed. It is not too late for Cory to achieve his dreams, but it is for Troy; thus, an undercurrent of jealousy colors his refusal to allow Cory to play football and go to college. In his warped sense of duty, Troy denies his son his own dream.

The Piano Lesson
Summary and Analysis

The Piano Lesson focuses on an African-American family's struggle to face the past and to embrace the future. The play is set in Pittsburgh in 1936, toward the end of the Great Depression. The drama takes places in the kitchen and parlor, and though the house is neat, "there is a lack of warmth and vigor." Dominating the residence is the ornately carved upright piano, which operates as both the play's central symbol and central conflict.

The play opens at dawn at the house, where Berniece Charles and her 11-year-old daughter live with Berniece's uncle, Doaker, a middle-aged railroad cook. The house is quiet until Berniece's brother, Boy Willie, shows up with his friend Lymon. Boy Willie is exuberant and highspirited and insists on waking everyone up, "disrupting the house." Berniece, 35, is still mourning her husband, who died three years ago, and is not pleased by her brother's arrival. Doaker, a quiet man who cooks for himself and plays solitaire, serves as the family's peacemaker.

Boy Willie and Lymon have driven up from Mississippi in Lymon's broken-down truck, ostensibly to sell watermelons. Boy Willie explains that Robert Sutter, the descendent of the slaveholders who once owned the Charles family's ancestors, mysteriously drowned in a well, and now Boy Willie has two weeks to earn the money so that he can buy the land from Sutter's brother. Boy Willie's real reason for the visit is to sell the piano, but Doaker warns him that Berniece will never sell it. Though Berniece does not play it, she also cannot let go of it, associating the piano with the memory of her murdered father and with her grief-stricken mother. The main focus of the play is the battle between

Berniece and Boy Willie over the piano, which represents their family history and also emerges as a symbol of slavery and the scars it inflicted on all African Americans.

Boy Willie's visit not only disturbs the quiet of the house, but it seems to literally awaken the dead: Berniece sees Sutter's ghost, who is calling for Boy Willie. When Boy Willie says that the Ghosts of Yellow Dog caused Sutter's death, Berniece accuses her brother of pushing Sutter into the well. The tension between the siblings increases when Berniece insinuates that Boy Willie is also responsible for the death of her husband, Crawley.

The story of the black migration to the North serves as the historical backdrop to the play. As a man who works on the trains, Doaker has seen many African Americans running from their past lives to discover freedom in the North, only to end up feeling disappointed and disillusioned. But for Avery, a preacher who wants to marry Berniece, the North provides opportunities. Though he works as an elevator operator, his dream is to secure a loan from the bank so he can establish his church.

Lymon also believes in the dream of the North: "They treat you better up here." Lymon is fleeing trouble with the law. After both Lymon and Boy Willie were imprisoned for supposedly stealing their boss's wood, a white man named Stovall paid $100 to secure Lymon's release, on the condition that he work for him. Instead of working, Lymon fled. Boy Willie, thus, is the only one who wants to return to the South. After he sells the piano, Boy Willie plans to ride the train back to Mississippi, insisting he will get his chance for economic freedom and independence there.

In scene 2, Wining Boy, Doaker's older brother, shows up. Wining Boy is a musician who found some success but now is broke and drinks to alleviate the pain of his failures. Meanwhile, Boy Willie and Lymon have been trying to sell watermelons, but the truck keeps breaking down; however, Boy Willie is happy because he now has the name of the white man who is interested in buying the piano.

In this scene, Doaker tells the story of the piano. Years ago, the slave owner Robert Sutter traded "one and a half" of his slaves (Doaker's grandmother Berniece and his father who was then nine years old) for a piano, an anniversary gift for his wife Miss Ophelia. At first, Miss Ophelia was delighted, but then, realizing how dependent she was on her slaves, she wanted them back. When the exchange was refused, Ophelia fell ill. So Sutter instructed Doaker's grandfather, the original Boy Willie and the plantation carpenter, to carve the pictures of his wife and son on the piano so that Miss Ophelia could look at them. Boy Willie ended up carving the Charles family history into the piano, a montage of scenes that collectively formed a slave narrative and celebrated the lives of his scattered family. Though Sutter was angry at Boy Willie for adding the scenes to the instrument, Ophelia was delighted and played the piano until she died.

Years later, Boy Charles (Berniece and Boy Willie's father) led his brothers, Doaker and Wining Boy, into the Sutter house to take back the piano. He felt the piano, as a record of their family history, rightfully belonged to them; if it remained under Sutter's control, then it seemed, symbolically, as if their family still belonged to him as well. The men safely hid the piano in the next county. However, a group of white men burned down Boy Charles's home and then stopped the train that he was on and lit the car on fire, burning Boy Charles and four transients alive. Over the years, the mysterious drownings of white men that occurred are said to be caused by the ghosts of the men who died on the Yellow Dog train. The play's repetition of events involving the piano and the similarity of family names creates an immediacy that unites the Sutters and Charleses across several generations.

Boy Willie and Berniece both acknowledge that their father died because of the piano, but they continue to argue over the piano's purpose. Boy Willie believes the piano will give the chance to assert his independence: "I'm going back and live my life the way I want to live it." Instead of running away, Boy Willie wants to secure his freedom on the same land where his family once worked as slaves. Berniece argues, "Money can't buy what that piano cost." For Berniece, the piano represents the suffering of the Charles family. Her ancestors were bartered like livestock for the piano, and her father's insistence on taking back the piano cost him his life and left her mother a lifetime of grief.

Their dispute over the piano leads to an argument about how Berniece's husband died. When Boy Willie and Lymon were confronted by white men for taking their boss's wood, they ran, but Crawley stayed and was killed. Boy Willie was shot in the stomach, and both he and Lymon were sentenced to prison. Berniece feels only resentment toward her brother. Blaming him for her husband's death, she lashes out and hits him, bringing the first act to an end.

Act 2 contains five scenes, and as the plot builds, the pace quickens, and the suspense is heightened. The following morning, Doaker tells Wining Boy that he has also seen Sutter's ghost and believes that Berniece should get rid of the piano, but Wining Boy sides with Berniece. Boy Willie and Lymon then enter, their pockets stuffed with money. They have been selling watermelons, and Boy Willie inflated the prices when he realized how easily the white customers would spend their money. In a comical moment, Wining Boy sells his silk "magic suit" to Lymon, and Lymon and Boy Willie go out to "find some women."

Scene 2 begins with Berniece and Avery. Avery wants to get married, but Berniece is not ready. Berniece not only guards the family history, but she also holds onto her grief, prompting Avery to ask, "How long you gonna carry Crawley with you, Berniece?" Berniece wants Avery to bless the house because her daughter, Maretha, has also seen Sutter's ghost. Though she lets her daughter play the piano, she does not tell Maretha its history: "I ain't gonna burden her with that piano."

In scene 3, Boy Willie comes home with a woman, but Berniece makes them leave, asserting her matriarchal power. Shortly after they go, Lymon comes in and gives Berniece a bottle of perfume. Wearing the magical suit, Lymon kisses Berniece, catching her off guard; it has been several years since she has experienced intimacy or allowed herself to feel vulnerable.

Boy Willie returns in scene 4 to tell Lymon that he has made a deal with the man to buy the piano. They try to move the instrument, but it is too heavy; it is not as easy as Boy Willie thought to get rid of the past.

Scene 5 is the final scene in the play. It begins with Boy Willie explaining the legend of the Ghosts of the Yellow Dog to Maretha. He believes that Berniece should tell her daughter the story of the piano's origin and instill in her a sense of familial pride. Not only do Berniece and Boy Willie view the past differently, but they hold contrasting ideas about their status in the world. Berniece, as a cleaning woman, believes that African Americans occupy the lowest rung of the socioeconomic ladder and tells her brother, "You right at the bottom with the rest of us." But Boy Willie wants Berniece to find hope for the future and encourages her to live freely instead of fearing white society or the past. Despite the obstacles facing him, Boy Willie will be his own master: "That's all I'm trying to do with that piano. Trying to put my mark on the road. Like my daddy done." Boy Willie wants to honor his sharecropper father by using the family heirloom to buy a piece of the American Dream.

Avery arrives to bless the house, and Lymon, whose date is waiting for him outside, agrees to help Boy Willie move the piano. Tension escalates, and Berniece comes downstairs with her husband's gun. Avery and Doaker try to get the brother and sister to calmly "talk this out." When Grace, Boy Willie's love interest, comes to the door suddenly, everybody senses Sutter's presence.

As Avery blesses the piano, Boy Willie mocks the blessing then begins yelling at Sutter's ghost, working "himself into a frenzy." The unseen ghost and Willie begin to wrestle in "a life and death struggle." Boy Willie is thrown to the bottom of the stairs repeatedly, and finally, he runs up the stairs with wild determination to physically battle the past, as Berniece now "realizes what she must do."

The past cannot be overcome by sheer brute force: The family must let the ancestral voices be heard. Berniece sits down at the piano and begins to play a song "intended as an exorcism and dress for battle." She calls out names of dead family members, asking for their help. When she is through, "a calm comes over the house." Sutter's ghost, a symbol of slavery, is quiet, and then they hear the rumbling of a train, symbolizing that the journey from the past to the present is over.

Boy Willie will take the train back home, but he tells his sister to keep playing the piano because Sutter's ghost can come back at any time. In the last line of the play, Berniece says, "Thank you," thereby letting go of the pain of the past and also reclaiming her connection to the family. The siblings are brought together through the family legacy and shared history.

Major Themes

The Piano Lesson covers the period in American history following the Great Depression, when many African Americans migrated north. Named for a painting by artist Romare Bearden, the play presents a provocative view of the burden of ancestry and the importance of legacy. In writing the work, Wilson explores what an individual does with his or her legacy. He chronicles the experience of African Americans by focusing on the importance of ancestral voices and family ties and evokes questions about freedom, ownership, and opportunity. The play also portrays how folklore and oral stories are African-American traditions that unite the past with the present.

The Power of African-American Legacy

The play centers on Berniece and Boy Willie's fight over their family legacy. For Berniece, the piano represents the memories of her family and her personal loss. Her mourning of the past and inability to engage with it have brought her life to a standstill. Boy Willie does not want to feel anguish over a painful past; rather he seeks to use his legacy as a positive means of securing his future. Instead of feeling weighted by the haunting legacy of slavery, Boy Willie thinks the legacy of African Americans should be used for new opportunities. Acquiring Sutter's land will validate his existence as a free man; as a landowner in the South, he will be able to usurp white power and rewrite family history.

In the end, Berniece, Boy Willie, and the other family members face their legacy, both the suffering of the past and the hope for the future. The piano links the Charles family to their ancestors, and when they call on the ancestors for help, they are able to find peace. By exorcising the ghost of slavery, they find a way to engage with the past and to move forward.

Oral Tradition in Black Culture

Folklore, legends, and ghost stories are all part of the Charles family's experience. Wilson weaves their stories and songs throughout the narrative, creating a narrative collage and tapping into the rich vein of black oral tradition. In both African and African-American cultures, oral tradition is a way of passing down memories, uniting generations, and connecting to a spiritual realm.

In *The Piano Lesson*, these oral traditions bring a divided family together. Doaker, the family historian, explains the legacy of the piano and its connection to the Charleses and the Sutters, while Wining Boy tells stories about the Ghosts of Yellow Dog. Boy Willie tells the story to Berniece's daughter, in order to keep the family legends alive among the youngest generation. As the characters recall family stories, they connect the present to the past and also find a way to locate themselves within a dominant society that alienates and pushes them to the fringe.

Music is also a way for the family to communicate. Various types of music are played on the piano—boogie woogie, the blues, and Berniece's anthem of exorcism—as a way to bring life or peace into the house. The men also bond when they sing a railroad song, which introduces another central theme of Wilson's— the intimacy and friendships among men. Singing, storytelling, and folklore are all important parts of the oral African-American tradition, and Wilson shows how the Charles family uses this kind of communication to remember the dead and to connect to the living.

CHARLES JOHNSON

Biography

CHARLES JOHNSON was born April 23, 1948, in Evanston, Illinois, the only child of Benny Lee and Ruby Elizabeth. His father did not attend high school, and both parents worked several jobs to support the family, while actively participating in the African Methodist Episcopalian Church. His mother was interested in the arts and literature, often bringing home discarded books from her cleaning jobs. Throughout his childhood and adolescence, Johnson's passion was drawing and visual arts. He attended Southern Illinois University, where he received his B.S. in 1971 and his M.A. in philosophy in 1973. He obtained his Ph.D. in philosophy from the State University of New York at Stony Brook in 1988.

Johnson first received attention in the 1960s as a political cartoonist, at a time when he was also involved in the Black Arts movement. He began placing his cartoons at 17, eventually selling more than 1,000 drawings to publications ranging from *Black World* to the *Chicago Tribune*. He published two collection of cartoons, *Black Humor* (1970) and *Half-Past Nation Time* (1972), and created a 52-part how-to-draw television series about cartooning on public television called *Charlie's Pad*. In the summer of 1967, Johnson began to practice Chinese martial arts and study Buddhism, which continue to play a major role in his life and art.

Inspired by the American writer John Gardner, whom he met when he was studying philosophy at SIU, Johnson began focusing on writing. His goal was to expose African-American literature to issues of Western and Eastern philosophy and to expand the category of black philosophical fiction. His first novel, *Faith and the Good Thing*, was published in 1974, when he was studying for a doctoral degree in philosophy. His other works of fiction and nonfiction include *Oxherding Tale* (1982); *The Sorcerer's Apprentice: Tales and Conjurations* (1986);

his dissertation, *Being and Race: Black Writing Since 1970* (1988); *Dreamer: A Novel* (1998), an imaginative treatment of Martin Luther King Jr.; *Soulcatcher* (2001); and *Turning the Wheel* (2003), a collection of essays about Buddhism. Johnson is a MacArthur "Genius" Fellow and a Guggenheim Fellowship recipient. He has written numerous essays on aesthetics and has given many lectures and interviews. He is currently the S. Wilson and Grace M. Pollock Endowed Professor of English at the University of Washington, where he has been teaching since 1976. He has also co-directed the Twin Tigers studio for martial arts in Seattle since 1986.

Johnson's most popular and critically acclaimed book, *Middle Passage*, was awarded the National Book Award in 1990. The narrative examines America's history of slavery and contrasts an African worldview with Western materialism. Johnson's philosophical background and Buddhist beliefs strongly influence his writing. In Johnson's view, the purpose of art is to challenge the fundamental ways we see the world, and he believes a writer must engage in philosophical debate. He follows his mentor John Gardner's ideas that a writer should create "moral fiction" and be committed to ethics. Johnson caused controversy in the updated 1995 introduction to his novel *Oxherding Tale*, when he seemed to criticize Alice Walker's *The Color Purple* for a negative portrayal of African-American males, viewing this as a moral issue. Themes of the nature of the self and personal identity and questions of liberation and morality run throughout his work. Johnson's novels and stories often blend philosophy, spirituality, humor, and political satire, while examining the black experience in America.

Middle Passage
Summary and Analysis

Middle Passage, which takes place in 1830, is made up of nine chapters that appear as the ship's logbook entries. The novel's narrator and the ship's biographer is Rutherford Calhoun, a newly freed bondsman slave from southern Illinois now living in New Orleans, a city "tailored to my taste for the excessive, exotic fringes of life." Calhoun is a hedonist, "drawn by nature to extremes" who "literally *hungered* . . . for life," as well as a scoundrel and petty thief, "living off others" and existing as "a social parasite." Calhoun is witty, intelligent, and well versed in the Bible and philosophy, as taught to him by his former owner, Reverend Chandler, who "hated slavery" and "out of Christian guilt" educated Calhoun and his brother. Throughout his narrative, Calhoun references philosophers and explores ideas about existence, freedom, and identity. Although this is a novel that exposes suffering and brutality, Johnson adds comical elements as well.

Calhoun writes the ship log entries after his trip on the *Republic* is over, when he is safely aboard the *Juno*. With the first sentence, he sets up the tale as an adventure and a tribulation and also ensures his survival: "But what lay ahead in Africa, then later on the open, endless sea, was, as I shall tell you, far worse than the fortune I'd fled in New Orleans." When the novel begins, Calhoun has been freed for a year and is now trapped in a life of pleasure and corruption. His only notion of freedom is how he can satisfy himself. Calhoun enjoys his bachelor lifestyle, and the reason he flees New Orleans is to free himself from potential wedlock.

His love interest, Isadora Bailey, is a Christian woman who is bookish and stable, "grounded, physically and metaphysically, in the land." She is a selfless, kind woman whose apartment is overrun with stray dogs and cats. Calhoun thinks "a smart man" should avoid love, and he fears that Isadora wants to change him into a "'gentleman of color.'" When Calhoun vows he will never get married, Isadora makes an arrangement with Philippe "Papa" Zeringue, a wealthy Creole gangster who offers to pay off Calhoun's debts if Calhoun marries Isadora the next day.

Feeling trapped, Calhoun leaves Isadora to go to a pub filled with drunken sailors, where he feels at home. There he meets Squibb, who tells him that he is shipping out the next day. After Squibb passes out from excessive intoxication, Calhoun steals his papers and climbs aboard the *Republic*, unaware at the time that he has stowed away on a slave ship. The *Republic* is associated with death imagery throughout the novel: "Not a ship but a kind of fantastic, floating Black Maria, a wooded sepulcher whose timbers moaned with the memory of too many runs of black gold between the New World and the Old." The ship, like the nation, is in a constant state of disrepair, trying to rebuild itself.

At sea, Calhoun is discovered by Peter Cringle, the first mate and quartermaster. Cringle is willing to let Calhoun stay on, but only after he meets with the captain. Cringle leads him to the captain's quarters, where the young cabin boy, Tommy O'Toole, is just leaving: Calhoun's first impression of Captain Ebenezer Falcon is that he has been raping Tommy. When Calhoun enters the cabin, he is greeted by a strange, high-pitched voice, and when he sees the owner of the voice, Calhoun is immediately repelled and fascinated. The infamous, feared Captain Ebenezer Falcon is a dwarf, standing only as high as Calhoun's hips. Falcon is a grotesque character, a strange, eccentric man, who wears steel-toed boots and writes in the nude. He is intelligent, philosophical, and dangerous.

Falcon represents the Captain Ahab character (from Herman Melville's novel *Moby-Dick*) who yearns for his own death: "yet, for all this obsession with survival, he had the air of a man who desperately wanted to die, which made his position on ship—his power over the others—all the more frightening." Falcon, the epitome of greed, is "that special breed of empire builder, explorer, and imperialist." He unnerves Calhoun when he happily tells him that they once ate a man on board.

Calhoun assists the good-natured alcoholic Squibb in the kitchen. The ship is squalid, roach infested, and "physically unstable." In Cringle's view, it is "worse than jail." The food is rotted and disgusting. Most of the men on board, when not on duty, stay drunk: "The whole Middle Passage, you might say, was one long hangover." The all-male crew resembles the clientele at the pubs in New Orleans, the ship weighed down by its hypermasculine inhabitants.

Unlike the rough crew, many of whom are criminals, Peter Cringle is an educated gentleman and at first seems out of place. Cringle feels guilty about his occupation but does nothing to stop what is morally reprehensible, symbolizing a white liberal who does not take action. Though Cringle feels concern for Tommy O'Toole, he does not protect the boy from Falcon's continuing sexual assaults. Cringle claims to not like slavery, yet he is an accomplice and describes human beings as "cargo." Like Falcon, Cringle is detached from the others, but he regrets his separation and blames his father for his choices.

Forty-one days later, in the third entry, the ship arrives at the trading post of Bangalang, and already Calhoun misses warmth, cleanliness, and Isadora. When he breaks into Falcon's cabin, he discovers "crates of plunder from every culture conceivable," and as he slips a few doubloons down the front of his shirt, he comes upon Falcon's journal, in which he discovers Falcon's background: Falcon is a mythical man who "made *himself* dangerous."

Falcon develops a friendship with Calhoun, holding long, mostly one-sided discussions about his philosophy that the strong are destined to rule the weak. Throughout the novel, Johnson weaves in contemporary modes of speech and contemporary cultural debates; for example, Falcon disagrees with the policy of affirmative action. Johnson's use of the modern reference is a way to criticize the social structures of the past that promoted racism, while also challenging contemporary society to alter the legacy of the past.

Falcon, who trusts no one on his crew, enlists Calhoun as his spy, his "Judas." When Falcon gives him, in exchange for a pistol, a ring that matches the one he wears, Calhoun feels as if "we were married." The irony is that Calhoun left New Orleans because he did not want to find himself in such a situation, but now he is like a "shipboard bride." As the critic Rudolph Byrd explains, "in stowing away on the *Republic* he has exchanged one species of bondage, wedlock, for another; life aboard a slave ship under the monomaniacal command of Captain Ebenezer Falcon" (114).

Calhoun's misgivings about being a part of a slave ship crew intensify. Unlike the others on the crew, he perceives the Allmuseri, the group of Africans being transported, as human beings, not cargo. The Allmuseri, a fictive creation, are the origins "of humanity itself." In looking at them, Calhoun realizes that he has never felt "such antiquity." The Africans' blank palms and absence of fingerprints set them apart from other people in the world. The opposite of Falcon, they have no ego; they want to feel harmonious with the world, not conquer it. The Allmuseri believe that the Americans are savages and that they are taking them to purgatory. Separated from their families, the Allmuseri are humiliated and treated "like cattle." On boarding the ship, they grow terrified. One woman throws her baby over the side so that it will not have to endure the ordeal ahead.

For the first time, Calhoun is deeply affected, and it "was then my hair started going white."

Falcon has brought not only the slaves on board but something else that "has no business in our world": a giant crate "big enough to carry a bull." When Tommy O'Toole comes into contact with it, he returns "with only half his mind." In trying to describe it, the boy speaks in various languages and poetically explains the magnificent, overpowering presence: "singer, listener, and song, light spilling into light, the boundaries of inside and outside, here and there, today and tomorrow."

In the fourth logbook entry, the *Republic* is homeward bound, taking the Allmuseri back to the United States. One of the leaders of the Allmuseri is Ngonyama, a quiet, observant, noble man. He learns some English from Calhoun and asks about the crew. Throughout the novel, Johnson subverts many racist stereotypes. In looking at the white crew, for example, Ngonyama wonders, "How do their families tell them apart?" playing on the stereotype that members of a racial or ethnic group physically resemble one another. From Ngonyama, Calhoun learns more about the Allmuseri, who seem to emit "a quiet magic," living in the present "ageless culture." They have no science but are a creative force, and their values seem to be derived from Hinduism, Buddhism, and Taoism.

One day Calhoun tosses a biscuit to Baleka, an Allmuseri girl, but her mother examines it and, seeing that it is moldy, throws it into the sea and scolds Calhoun. To make up for it, he later shares his dinner with the girl, Baleka, and considers it "a major mistake," because from then on the girl and mother expect him to share all of his food. But he and Baleka soon grow "inseparable." When a violent storm knocks the ship off course, it washes half of the Allmuseri children and women, Baleka's mother among them, into the sea. The crew, terrified that the ship is going down, prays to God, and Calhoun notices only Ngonyama "was dry. . . . He was coolness itself." He mysteriously warns Calhoun to "lay below" tomorrow.

Cringle recruits Calhoun to join him and a few others in a mutiny. They plan to take over the ship and then leave Falcon marooned. Fearing retaliation from the ship's investors, the men want Calhoun to take the blame because he can disappear "like he's always done, believin' in nothin', belongin' to nobody, driftin' here and there." In his life before traveling the Middle Passage, Calhoun existed only for himself. As the critic Gary Storhoff attests, "Rutherford Calhoun is literally the American self-made man, who creates, then revises, himself as he goes along (much as the crew rebuilds the *Republic*). . . . For Rutherford, identity itself is only a performance" (158). One reason Calhoun left New Orleans is because he did not want the fixed identity that he believed marriage would give him: He wanted freedom instead.

Calhoun admits that he is a liar: "As a general principle and mode of operation during my days as a slave, I always lied." Yet he also establishes a trust with the reader and is not an unreliable, deliberately deceptive narrator. Calhoun agrees to be a part of the mutiny and drinks from the cup of the crew's shared blood, only then to reveal the mutiny scheme to Falcon. Calhoun is caught between the rival camps of the *Republic*. He represents the "middle" position, between Falcon and the crew and between the crew and the Allmuseri. He admits, "I could no longer find my loyalties." He does not trust the crew or Falcon. The ship "was a coffin" that will go down unless "someone played a trump. . . . I realized that I held that card." Calhoun must choose between the philosophies of Falcon and the Allmuseri: Falcon, symbolizing imperialism, believes the strongest are destined to rule the weakest; in contrast, the Allmuseri believe that individual ownership is unnatural.

When Calhoun looks at the Allmuseri, he is reminded of his brother. In the fifth logbook entry, Calhoun tells the story of his brother Jackson and why he felt betrayed by him and by his father, who "cut and run." On his deathbed, Master Chandler planned to leave everything to Calhoun and Jackson, but Jackson refused the idea of ownership. Instead, he wanted everything to be evenly divided among everyone who had ever worked on the estate and for the rest of the money to be given to a college in Oberlin, Ohio, that "helps Negroes on their way north." Calhoun, outraged, was left with about "forty dollars" and the "Family Bible and his bedpan." Though Chandler claimed he hated slavery, he still profited from it and displayed racist condescension. By refusing to inherit Chandler's estate, Jackson refused to be a part of the legacy of slavery and, like the Allmuseri, refused ownership.

After thinking about his brother, Calhoun knows he must put his faith in the Allmuseri and must act out of concern for Baleka. Transformed and no longer thinking about himself, he wants to help her: "I could not let her die, a dark pawn, caught between Falcon and the ship's proletariat." In telling the story of his brother, Calhoun realizes that Jackson lived a selfless life, a life of transcendence, and Calhoun is no longer bitter. He gives Ngonyama the key he stole from Falcon, in the hope that it will unlock their chains.

In the novel's sixth logbook entry, Calhoun's transformation continues, with a deepening of his commitment to humanity. When one of the Allmuseri youth dies, Calhoun is instructed to throw the body overboard, but he hesitates. He identifies with the young African. If he does not throw the boy off the ship, he betrays himself to the crew, but if he does, then he will be connected with the evils of slavery. The crew grows impatient, so Calhoun does what he is told. But when he throws the corpse overboard, the leg breaks off in his hand, and he is covered with the rotting flesh and blood of the boy. Marked with the traces of his grave act, his hand "no longer felt like my own. Something in me said it would never be clean again." He picks up the knife as if to cut off his own hand, but Ngonyama stops him. This is the catalyst for Calhoun's change, when he cries "for all the sewage I carried in my spirit, my failures and crimes, foolish hopes and vanities." In order to evolve, Calhoun must forgive himself.

Chaos soon erupts on the ship. The different factions are fighting, and cannons are being fired. The Allmuseri take over the ship. They want to kill Cringle, who symbolizes the horrors that all Africans suffered in the Middle Passage. Diamelo, in particular, wants revenge and justice. Calhoun is a sympathetic witness to their testimony about the brutality they have suffered, but he does not want to be a part of any more killing. He convinces them not to kill Cringle and offers him to be their slave instead. When Cringle accuses him of taking the wrong side, Calhoun exclaims, "I'm not on anybody's side. I'm just trying to keep us alive."

In the seventh logbook entry, Calhoun speaks with Falcon, who is imprisoned by the Allmuseri. He wants Calhoun to make the journal entries now, to tell the truth of what happened on the ship. After Calhoun leaves, Falcon shoots himself.

Now that the Allmuseri have taken over the ship, Diamelo imposes new rules: The white crew must learn their stories, use Allmuseri medicine, and lower their eyes when their women pass. However, Calhoun observes, "On both sides, African and American, survivors of the revolt felt too battered to embrace an entirely new regime." The crew and the Allmuseri are sick and dying, and the ship is lost at sea, "a phantom ship." Cringle feels unable to direct the ship back to the United States: "The heavens are all wrong." Critic Gary Storhoff suggests, "By actually living the life of a captured African, Cringle begins to understand through his own experience the suffering that the slaves had to endure, and though he attempts to steer the ship toward American ports, he fails because his cosmos is symbolically altered by his servitude" (175).

Meanwhile, Calhoun is able to move beyond his own self-interests and show more concern for others. He reaches a new understanding about identity and the true meaning of freedom:

> for in myself I found nothing I could rightly call Rutherford Calhoun, only pieces and fragments of all the people who had touched me, all the places I had seen, all the homes I had broken into. The 'I' that I was, was a mosaic of many countries, a patchwork of others and objects stretching backward to perhaps the beginning of time.

When Ngonyama confronts him, asking why he came onto this slave ship, Calhoun is overcome with remorse.

It is now Calhoun's turn to feed the "dangerous, shape-shifting god of the Allmuseri." The god seems to represent an individual's desire, secret, or past. For Falcon, it was "a witty conversationalist . . . though prone to periods of self-pity and depression." The deity is also representative of the shifting states of identity and nationality. When Calhoun confronts it, it presents itself to Calhoun "in the form of the one man with whom I had bloody, unfinished business . . . my father, the fugitive Riley Calhoun."

In the eighth logbook entry, Calhoun must face the abandonment of his father. Though he has always hated his father for leaving him, he now considers his father as a frightened slave, running away and getting killed just a few miles from Chandler's place. In order to evolve, Calhoun must let go of the hatred he feels for his father: "The hate that Calhoun feels for his father is an impediment to Calhoun's psychological and spiritual growth" (Byrd 134). Finally empathizing with his father, Calhoun collapses under the emotional weight of this revelation.

When Calhoun wakes up three days later, his hair completely white, Squibb is feeding him meat, which he informs him is actually Cringle, who also transformed himself. By offering his dying body to the others, both Africans and Americans, Cringle changed into a selfless person. Similarly, Squibb, once a slave to alcohol, now offers to help everyone on the ship. Calhoun finally feels at home with the transformation of the crew and with the community of the Allmuseri, who are also changing. The horrors they have experienced on the ship "were subtly reshaping their souls." Identity, nationality, and race emerge not as fixed things but as constantly evolving and growing elements of identity. Calhoun realizes they are "No longer Africans, yet not Americans either. Then what? And of what were they now capable?"

An explosion rocks the ship, when Diamelo misfires a cannon. The ship catches on fire, and the crew members fall into the Atlantic, drowning. In the last entry of the ship's log, Calhoun, Squibb, and three children, including Baleka, are saved and taken aboard the magnificent *Juno*, "a floating gin palace." Recovering from shock, Calhoun spends the days writing the story of the *Republic* in the ship's logbook: "I found a way to make my peace with the recent past by turning it into Word." He is changed physically (he has lost his hair and is rickety and unstable, "a wreck of the Republic") and emotionally. He feels like a father to Baleka, and he has freed himself of the greed and hypermasculinity of the ship. He now weeps often and accepts Baleka's caretaking.

Calhoun then finds out that Philippe Zeringue is on the ship and plans to marry Isadora. Earlier, Calhoun was shocked to find out that Papa was one of the investors in the *Republic*. Papa is well respected in the black community, and if people found out that he was one of the owners of a slave ship, his reputation would be destroyed. Calhoun confronts Zeringue in front of his henchman, Santos, and blackmails him into giving each of the Allmuseri children a full endowment, at the same time forcing him to leave Isadora and Calhoun alone.

Isadora sees that Calhoun has given up his selfish ways: "You don't look or sound the same." He apologizes to her and asks her to marry him. The book ends with Calhoun and Isadora in bed together, with Isadora trying to seduce him in a comical scene. However, still traumatized by the memories of what he witnessed, Calhoun realizes that sensual pleasure is not what he wants: "I wanted our futures blended, not our limbs." Calhoun is transformed and feels "the difference in me" as they "gently crossed the Flood, and countless seas of suffering." At the end of his physical and spiritual journey, Calhoun rejects his former life. He plans to return to Illinois with Isadora and Baleka: Transformed, he has discovered freedom in selflessness and the promotion of harmony.

Major Themes

Middle Passage is a nautical tale, an adventure story, a slave narrative, a historical novel, and a philosophical inquiry. The main subject of the novel is the Middle Passage, and the dominating theme is the quest for true freedom. By focusing on the dynamics between a white crew, a freed black man, and African slaves, Johnson explores the meaning of freedom as well as the construction of race. He subverts or overturns racial stereotypes and myths and challenges readers to think about race in new ways.

The novel is also a testament to the damaging legacy of the slave trade and imperialism: Johnson examines how knowledge of the past can transform the present. The contrast in the philosophies of Falcon and the Allmuseri is a major theme: Do those who conquer the weak prevail, or will humanity find peace once people free themselves of their egotism and will for power? The novel investigates themes of existence and identity, depicting both personal and national identity as continuous, evolving creations. Furthermore, *Middle Passage* explores themes of masculinity by focusing on relationships between fathers and sons, the rivalry between brothers, and the friendships among white, African, and African-American men.

Facing America's History

Johnson writes about a part of history that many Americans do not know much about or would like to forget. The Middle Passage refers to the central part of the slave trade voyage across the Atlantic, between Africa, the West Indies, and the slaveholding states. The conditions were brutal: Ships contained several hundred slaves, with male captives chained in pairs. Between 9 million and 12 million Africans were victims of the slave trade, and many died on the Middle Passage of starvation or disease. Through the story of the crew and the Africans aboard the *Republic*, Johnson confronts the varying shame or denial attached to this brutal history. One of the themes of the novel is how Americans must face and learn from the past in order to evolve.

The novel explores the damaging effects of slavery and imperialism, which undermine democratic principles. Falcon, as conqueror and plunderer, symbolizes imperialism; he thrives from greed, and his "burning passion was the manifest destiny of the United States to Americanize the entire planet." Falcon's passion for conquering destroys other cultures, families, communities, and a sense of harmony in the world. Rather than take responsibility for this havoc, Falcon kills himself, but his terrible legacy will continue: "Centuries would pass whilst the Allmuseri lived through the consequences of what he had set in motion; he would be with them, I suspected, for eons, like an ex-lover, a despised husband, a rapist."

Falcon is the most extreme embodiment of the imperialist system, but Johnson examines how the history of the United States has been tarnished by its legacy of slavery. Cringle and Reverend Chandler say that they are opposed to slavery, but both contribute to slavery's existence and benefit from its profits. Calhoun must also grapple with his own guilt when he throws the dead African off the ship and his hand is literally stained with blood: He is no longer innocent. This is a significant moment in which Calhoun realizes that even his small action contributes to the thriving and furthering of slavery. Papa Zeringue also contributes to and fuels the machinery of slavery by funding the slave ship. The ship itself emerges as a critique of America's involvement in this brutality. The critic Rudolph P. Byrd points out the irony in the name of the ship, the *Republic*: "Johnson invites us to evaluate and to remain cognizant of the irony, jeopardy, contradictions, and failures of the republic called the United States of America, a republic in the 1830s that aspires to realize the practice of democracy while also tolerating and sheltering the continued growth of slavery" (111).

American history should not be ignored or forgotten, Johnson is suggesting, even in all of its brutality. On the slave ship, Calhoun ponders what it means to be an American: "this land of refugees and former indentured servants, religious heretics and half-breeds, whoresons and fugitives . . . was all I could rightly call home, then aye: I was of it." Although *Middle Passage* is a novel about Calhoun and his transformation, it is also a story about America's national identity; like Calhoun, the country is in a state of constant revision. The knowledge of America's past, of both its wrongdoings and its successes, can lead to a national and personal transformation.

The Meaning of Freedom

One of the novel's main themes is Calhoun's quest for freedom. By setting the novel on a slave ship and in New Orleans, Johnson raises many challenging questions about the true nature of freedom. For instance, in New Orleans freed blacks live alongside a slave market. One of the issues Calhoun faces is how to live as a free black man in an era of slavery. Calhoun is set apart from the all-white crew, and yet he is also not like the Africans. His position, caught in the middle, while traveling the Middle Passage, is a cause of confusion. When they are at the trading post, Squibb advises Calhoun to lay low, because others will view him as an African. But Cringle disagrees and says the Allmuseri are "not like you either, though you are black." Ngonyama tells Calhoun that the Allmuseri "are your brothers," but Calhoun feels like an outsider: "Yes, I was black, as they were, but they had a common bond I could but marvel at." He would like to be a part of this harmonious community but feels separate because he is not at peace with himself.

This examination of freedom leads to many other important themes concerning race and identity. Calhoun is shocked and confused when he finds out that Zeringue would "buy and sell slaves when he himself was black? Was this not the greatest betrayal of all?" Papa is a free black man who enslaves other blacks; ironically, Falcon, as a free white male, "was no freer than the Africans," as he was partly enslaved to Zeringue.

Johnson explores many different forms of slavery. Though Calhoun is a freed black man living in New Orleans, he is a slave to a life of petty crime and sensual pleasures. He believes he is escaping the shackles of marriage but then finds himself trapped in a brutal system of slavery and imperialism. Squibb is a slave to alcohol, and Falcon is a slave to greed. Papa Zeringue is similarly trapped by his love of money and need to uphold his reputation.

Only the Allmuseri, who embody many Buddhist tenets and beliefs, are free because they do not desire or want. Though they are slaves, in many ways they are more free than any of the crew. Once Calhoun transforms, by facing and letting go of his past and by caring for and acting selflessly toward Baleka, he begins to find the true freedom the Allmuseri possess. After the Middle Passage, as the critic Byrd explains, Calhoun's "preoccupation with power, pleasure, and materialism did not make sense" (137), and only then can he experience true freedom. He has transformed from a "scoundrel" to a person who truly cares about others.

GLORIA NAYLOR

Biography

GLORIA NAYLOR was born January 25, 1950, in New York City to Roosevelt and Alberta McAlpin Naylor, the first of three daughters. Although she grew up in the city, her parents had been sharecroppers in Mississippi, and the communal voice in her work and storytelling style was influenced by the stories she heard from parents and relatives. In New York, her father was employed as a transit worker and her mother was a telephone operator. Her mother had little education but loved to read and passed this love of books to her daughter. In 1963, the family moved to Queens, to a more middle-class neighborhood, and that same year, Naylor's mother became a Jehovah's Witness. Later, Naylor followed in her footsteps, with a seven-year stint as lay minister and missionary.

Naylor worked as a switchboard operator while taking classes at Medgar Evers College, then transferred to Brooklyn College and majored in English. In 1977, she read her first novel by an African-American woman, Toni Morrison's *The Bluest Eye*, which gave her the courage to write. Naylor began writing fiction and submitted a story to *Essence*; the editor advised her to continue writing. While at Brooklyn College, she started writing her first novel, *The Women of Brewster Place*. After graduating with her B.A. in 1981, she attended Yale University where she obtained an M.A. in Afro-American studies.

The Women of Brewster Place was published in 1982 and won the American Book Award for first novel. The novel was turned into a television mini-series five years later, starring Oprah Winfrey as Mattie Michael. Naylor's other books include *Linden Hills* (1986), which she first wrote as her master's thesis at Yale; *Mama Day* (1988); *Bailey's Café* (1992); *The Men of Brewster Place* (1998); and a memoir, *1996* (2005). Naylor has taught at several colleges, including George Washington, Princeton, New York, Boston, and Cornell universities. She is the founder of One Way Productions, an independent film company, and is involved in a literacy program in the Bronx.

Naylor's novels are interrelated, connecting to one another with repeating characters and settings. She often uses events and people from her personal life and also draws extensively on the Bible, Shakespeare, and Dante. In *Linden Hills*, for example, she portrays a world in which black Americans have achieved status and power but have lost their souls, using Dante's *The Inferno* as an allegorical structure. *Mama Day* is a reassessment of Shakespeare's *The Tempest*; Naylor's treatment depicts a female, African-American version of the play's protagonist, Prospero.

Naylor's novels depict the richness and diversity of the African-American experience. She came of age during the turbulent 1960s and 1970s and often situates her novels within the various social and political moments defining twentieth-century America. Naylor is known for her strong depictions of the empowerment of black women. Her most famous work, *The Women of Brewster Place*, celebrates the strength of the black female experience, a major theme in her work. Community and the creation of sanctuaries are other important themes. For example, in *Bailey's Café*, the café offers respite for those who have been battered by the outside world, and in *The Women of Brewster Place*, the women, through friendship, offer one another refuge from their impoverished surroundings.

The Women of Brewster Place
Summary and Analysis

The Women of Brewster Place is made up of seven interlocking stories that describe a community of African-American women living in Brewster Place, a deteriorating housing development in a large, unnamed American city. The women represent the diversity of the African-American female experience, and yet, because they live in a sexist, racist society, they also experience many of the same struggles.

By using Langston Hughes's poem "Harlem" from his "Montage of a Dream Deferred" as the epilogue, Naylor establishes one of the novel's major themes: The dreams of these women have been deferred or postponed. The novel is framed by "Dawn" and "Dusk": the birth and near death of Brewster Place. The housing development, "the bastard child," was originally viewed as a sign of the city's new prosperity after World War II. But its first inhabitants, European immigrants, were ignored by the city, and Brewster Place turned into the typical urban space that is home to impoverished families. For traffic purposes, the street was walled off, so that Brewster Place became a dead end, a symbol of the ways the women's lives are restricted.

Brewster Place's third generation—African-American women—arrive as a result of difficult times, and they stay because they have no other choices. These women may have literally reached the dead end, but they do not give up hope. The women are "hard-edged, soft-centered, brutally demanding, and easily pleased. . . . They came, they went, grew up, and grew old beyond their years." Though Brewster Place is in decay, the women hold the place together. The image of the phoenix rising symbolizes their hope: "Like an ebony phoenix, each in her own time and with her own season had a story."

The first chapter, taking place in the winter, focuses on Mattie Michael, the community's matriarch and surrogate mother. A middle-aged woman, she provides moral stability for the community. She is wise, kind, strong, and accepting. Mattie arrives at Brewster Place in the 1970s on a snowy evening because she has nowhere else to go, losing the home she "had exchanged thirty years of her life to pay for." Mattie thinks she smells sugarcane but realizes that is impossible—it is a memory of her life in Tennessee.

Naylor then launches into an extended flashback. Most of this chapter, which covers a 30-year period, is occupied with this flashback. Mattie grew up in rural Tennessee, a place that holds some of her fondest as well as most painful memories. At 20 years old, she is seduced by a charming womanizer, "cinnamon-red" Butch Fuller, a welcome contrast to "deadpan Fred Watson," the only man her father approves of her dating. Butch represents freedom and openness, and he leads her to a patch where "the deep green basil and wild thyme formed a fragrant blanket on a mossy earth." After Mattie reveals that she is pregnant, her religious father stops speaking to her, eventually relenting and telling her that, as long as she marries Fred Watson, he will forgive her. When Mattie refuses to tell him who the father of her baby is, he flies into a rage and beats her with a broomstick. He does not stop until his wife pulls a shotgun on him; when he sees what he has done, he weeps.

Mattie takes a bus to stay with her childhood friend Etta in an unnamed city. After the baby (whom she names Basil as a reminder of the freedom of that day) is born, Etta, the wanderer, leaves, but Mattie stays, working on an assembly line. The despair of the "cramped boarding house room," is revealed when a rat climbs into Basil's crib and bites his lip. Devastated, Mattie leaves the next day in search of a new home, avoiding the white neighborhoods and the "neatly manicured back neighborhoods"; both her blackness and her status as an unwed mother limit her possibilities. Confused, scared, and dazed, she walks around until she is stopped by an old woman asking if she is lost. The woman looks white, but "it was a black voice." Throughout the novel, Naylor describes her characters in various shades and skin tones, depicting the diversity of a race and also questioning the simple divisions of black and white.

Miss Eva invites Mattie inside, offering her a home and friendship for the next 30 years. When Mattie goes to sleep that first Saturday night, she awakes on a Sunday morning, but many years have passed. Now Basil and Ciel, Miss Eva's granddaughter, are rambunctious children. Miss Eva is ornery yet warm and refuses Mattie's offer to pay rent, telling her to save her money. The only tension arises when Miss Eva tries to warn Mattie that she is too overprotective of her son. Mattie overindulges him, her love for him without limits, which later will cost her.

A few years after they move in, Eva dies, and Ciel is taken away by her parents. Mattie and Basil live in the house alone, and he becomes a spoiled 30-year-old man, "gulping coffee and shoving oatmeal into his mouth." Basil does not appreciate his mother's hard work—she has held two jobs in order to pay for the house. Mattie never taught him to confront the consequences of his behavior, and one night their world is turned upside down. Basil is accused of killing a man in a bar-room brawl. For 30 years, Basil and his selfish needs have dictated the course of Mattie's life; she will do anything for her son. Basil refuses to take the blame and shows no remorse; he exaggerated his fears of spending time in jail, telling Mattie that he heard a rat under his bed, a fierce reminder of the rodent she found biting him when he was a baby. Instead of taking the lawyer's advice to let Basil remain in jail for two more weeks until the trial, Mattie posts bail, offering up her house as collateral. Basil comes home for two weeks. Instead of freely occupying his time like he usually does, he helps his mother around the house and stays close by, and Mattie "reveled in his presence." But days before he is to appear in court, Basil flees. Broke and alone as a result, Mattie ends up at Brewster Place.

The next section focuses on Etta Mae Johnson, Mattie's childhood friend from Tennessee. Etta seeks out an exciting, fast-paced life. Functioning as Mattie's foil or opposite, Etta goes from place to place and from man to man. The other residents disapprove of her, but Etta feels no need to hide who she is and returns to Brewster Place that summer in a vinyl-topped Cadillac, after having a fling with a wealthy, married man. Etta is unconventional and strong. Even growing up, she never displayed the submissive attitude toward whites that was expected, nor is she submissive to men. Thus, "America wasn't ready for her yet."

The music of Billie Holiday, whom Etta once heard sing, helps her deal with hardship and rejection, and the lyrics act as commentary on her life. After she leaves the South, for example, pursued by angry white men, the lyrics of "Strange Fruit," a song about lynching, enter her mind: "Black bodies swinging / In the Southern breeze." When she returns to the gossiping community of Brewster Place, she is comforted by Holiday's "Ain't Nobody's Business If I Do."

Mattie wants Etta to settle down and find a nice, church-going man. So Etta agrees to attend service with her at the Canaan Baptist Church, a forbidding church where people "still worshipped God loudly." Etta, wearing a red dress, feels unmoved by the message but takes interest in the guest preacher, Reverend Moreland T. Woods. He functions as a stereotype of the womanizing preacher. Naylor's vivid description of Woods's sermon highlights his sexual presence and appeal: "he would have to push and pound" the congregation, his chest "heaving in long spasms," and after he is through, the congregation is left "limp and spent."

The reverend sees Etta right away, and the two engage in a flirtatious cat-and-mouse game. Etta convinces herself, in a fantasy, that Reverend Moreland T. Woods would want to marry her, rejecting Mattie's warning: "Can't you see what he's got in mind?" Mattie is right—the reverend only wants physical intimacy with Etta. The next morning, after he drops her off at Brewster Place, Etta feels tired, and she looks at the walled-in end of the street and thinks, "I'll never get out." Her experience with Woods is familiar, but for the first time, she is defeated by it, and if her neighbors had seen her, "This middle-age woman in the wrinkled dress and wilted straw hat would have been a stranger to them." Etta then notices that Mattie's light is on, and she is playing Billie Holiday: Etta has someone waiting for her after all.

The third chapter focuses on Kiswana Browne, a young woman from a middle-class black family in Linden Hills, who, unlike most of the other women, chooses to live at Brewster Place so that she can be with "her people." Kiswana is looking out her sixth-floor window daydreaming, when she sees her mother approaching the door. This part of the novel focuses on generational differences between mother and daughter, with references to the civil rights movement and the renewed focus in the 1970s of African Americans reclaiming their roots.

Whereas Mrs. Brown is mature and articulate, Kiswana is young, idealistic, and naive. She wants to be an activist but does not really understand what this entails. She takes on the African name Kiswana, though her mother still calls her Melanie, and she drops out of college because she sees it as boringly conventional and "counter-revolutionary." Beyond her ideas and abstract notions, however, she does not take any real actions that would help the women of Brewster Place.

Her mother supports her daughter's fight for better social conditions and civil rights for African Americans but argues that her daughter needs to get an education and to work within the system in order to change it. Kiswana resents everything her mother stands for; in a climactic scene, Kiswana says she would rather be dead than be like her mother. Her mother grabs her and tells her that by rejecting her given name, she is rejecting her mother's attempt to honor her strong, brave grandmother. Ironically, Mrs. Brown educates her daughter in black pride. Her mother's speech illuminates for Kiswana that she is not "breaking" any "new trails," and she realizes that her mother is "the woman she had been and was to become." Kiswana has learned to listen and to appreciate her mother, yet both realize they still hold very different viewpoints.

The next chapter focuses on Lucielia Louise Turner, known as Ciel, Miss Eva's granddaughter. Mattie is like a second mother to her, and Ciel relies on her for support. Ceil is trying to hold her family together, but her common-law husband, Eugene, has deserted her and their daughter, Serena. This chapter starts off with an angry Eugene, who admits he is not going to his child's funeral. The chapter then moves into flashback, to tell Ciel's story leading up to the funeral.

After leaving for a year, Eugene returns. Ciel hopes that this time he will stay. However, when Ciel is revealed to be pregnant, Eugene becomes angry and resentful that they will have another mouth to feed. Eugene is verbally abusive, and to show off his power, he refuses to let Mattie baby-sit Serena. Despite Eugene's poor treatment of her, Ciel wants him to stay. Feeling she has no other choice, she has an abortion. She hopes this will ease Eugene's worries; however, not long after, he tells her he is leaving to take a job in another state.

Devastated, Ciel does not tell him that she had an abortion for him, explaining rather that he cannot go because she loves him. As they argue, Serena, left alone to play in the other room, sticks a fork into an electrical outlet and is killed. This story suggests that Ciel's excessive focus on Eugene led to her daughter's death, though the accident occurred by coincidence. Ciel has lost everything she loved, and at the funeral, "Ciel's whole universe existed in the seven feet of space between herself and her child's narrow coffin." Ciel gives up on life because she was "simply tired of hurting." When Mattie realizes that Ciel, bedridden and despondent, wants to die, she rushes in and takes her in her arms and rocks her. This is one of the novel's climaxes, in which Mattie's loving arms save a woman from death. When Mattie washes her, it is a symbol of baptism and new life. When Ciel finally expresses her extreme grief at the death of her daughter, it is a release; now she is on her way to healing, and the narrative suggests that she will survive and grow stronger.

The fifth chapter is about Cora Lee, a woman who has seven children by mostly different fathers and keeps having them because she loves babies. As a child, she wanted a doll every Christmas and had her first real baby during her sophomore year of high school. With Cora Lee, Naylor examines the prejudiced representation of the "welfare mother." Cora Lee, supported by welfare and food stamps, spends her afternoons watching soap operas and taking care of her children. Cora Lee is a strong parent to them—protective, caring, kind—but she neglects them as well, wondering, "Why couldn't they just stay like this—so soft and easy to care for?" She raises them on her own, using men who come and go, "shadows," for sexual encounters because her only experiences with long-term relationships with men were negative. One man physically abused her, fracturing her jaw, abuse she endured until he complained about her baby; then, she sent him on his way.

When Kiswana arrives to inform Cora Lee that one of her sons was going through the garbage, Cora Lee is more perplexed by the interruption than by the news. This scene, in which Kiswana, obviously disturbed, tries to converse with Cora Lee, also reveals the change in Kiswana's character. No longer daydreaming about the tenants, Kiswana is instead interacting with them. When she invites Cora Lee to bring her children to the park to see her boyfriend Abshu's all-black production of *A Midsummer Night's Dream*, Cora Lee at first hesitates, worried the kids will embarrass her, but she finally agrees. It seems that Kiswana's obvious remark that babies grow up seems to suddenly register with Cora Lee.

The night of the play, Cora Lee works in a frenzy, washing and mending the children's clothes, combing their hair, and getting them ready for the play. Naylor's choice of *A Midsummer Night's Dream*, William Shakespeare's playful fantasy, is significant; as Cora Lee watches, she conjures a new resolve that she will become more active in her children's lives. She is surprised by how well behaved they are, and when her son, whom she has belittled and labeled an "ass," asks if he will grow up to look like the character Bottom, wearing donkey ears, she feels guilty. That night, she bathes them and puts them into bed with a kiss, saying, "this had been a night of wonders." The end of the chapter suggests the fantasy will not last, however, as she enters her bedroom, where a "shadow" is waiting for her.

"The Two" is the only chapter without a woman's name in the title. It focuses on Theresa and Lorraine, a lesbian couple who are ostracized by the women of Brewster Place. Naylor immediately sets them up as "the other" by describing how they, still unnamed, are viewed by the community. At first they are liked, until the women find out they "were that way," and then the community creates a wall between them that ends in tragedy.

The women are not economically deprived but come to Brewster Place to escape the gossip of residents in more affluent neighborhoods. Though Theresa, strong and unapologetic about who she is, does not care what others think or say, Lorraine wants to be accepted by the Brewster Place women. She attends the tenant association meeting at Kiswana's and is confronted by Miss Sophie, "official watchman for the block," who unleashes a homophobic diatribe.

Etta rises to Lorraine's defense, but it is the drunken janitor, Ben, who stops Sophie's hateful words. He and Lorraine strike up an unlikely friendship, and, for the first time, the story of Ben's past is revealed. Once a sharecropper, he lived with his wife and physically disabled daughter, who worked as the housekeeper for the white property owner, who required that she spend the night. When she revealed to her parents that he was having sex with her, her mother did not believe her, and Ben did not know how to help her. Unable to protect his daughter, she eventually ran off to become a prostitute in Memphis. Ben turned to drinking, the only way to forget and alleviate his guilt. Now, Lorraine, ostracized from her family, has symbolically returned to the guilty father. Through her friendship with Ben, Lorraine seems to become a stronger, more independent woman.

Still, the community's ostracisim and distance and Sophie's constant harassment begin to wear Theresa and Lorraine down, and they often erupt into arguments. One of the major conflicts between them concerns sexuality and identity. Theresa insists that, as lesbians, they are different from the others and should not try to fit in, but Lorraine believes that her sexuality does not define her. Naylor refrains from making judgments, allowing each woman's point to stand.

One night, for the first time, Lorraine goes to a party without Theresa. On the way home, she takes a shortcut through an alley, where she is attacked by a young man named C.C. and his gang. Naylor suggests that societal forces have shaped the teenagers, who rule the alley. C.C. views Lorraine as a threat to his manhood, and he leads the brutal attack. Lorraine attempts to stop them, uttering "please," but it is ineffective in stopping the brutal rape. The next morning, dazed and bloodied, she hears a sound; disoriented, she picks up a loose brick, and makes a final desperate lunge at the person approaching. Mistaking Ben for the rapists, she strikes Ben with the brick. Ben's death symbolizes the death of the father who failed his daughter. Lorraine then dies in Mattie's arms, although this time, Mattie, the surrogate mother, is too late.

The characters come together in "The Block Party," although it is only in a dream. Most of the chapter is a telling of Mattie's dream, in which the women of Brewster Place find resolution, solace, and vindication. Ciel returns, happy and in a new relationship, and reveals she dreamed of Lorraine, a woman she never met but who reminds her of herself. Kiswana has inspired the others to file a lawsuit against the landlord. Etta dances with a young man, regaining her youth. Only Cora Lee seems unchanged—pregnant again. But it is Cora Lee who realizes there is still blood on the bricks where Lorraine and Ben died, and she begins to remove them. Soon the other women join in: "Women flung themselves against the wall, chipping away at it with knives, plastic forks, spiked shoe heels, and even bare hands." When Cora hands Theresa a brick, Cora says "Please. Please," and Theresa recoils, saying, "Don't ever say that!" The word *please*, Lorraine's sole utterance in trying to prevent her rapists' attack, denies a woman's power. Theresa, now a part of the community, throws the brick and it shatters into green smoke.

In this climactic scene, the women destroy the wall and experience a symbolic baptism, as "the rain exploded around their feet in a fresh downpour and the cold waters beat on the top of their heads—almost in perfection with the beating of their hearts." But when Mattie wakes, the sun is shining. Naylor provides a dreamlike vision of what needs to happen among the women, but the reader does not see the actual block party. The novel ends as it begins, with a description of Brewster Place, which has been condemned and its residents evicted. Though it is dying, its daughters are not; they are still alive and dreaming, moving on to face a new future.

Major Themes

Naylor focuses on the strength of the African-American community and the prevailing love of women. Though dreams are frustrated and go unrealized, the characters have not given up. Though the women live on a dead-end street in an impoverished housing complex, their support and friendship allow them to build a sanctuary of hope and to escape the grimness of their surroundings. A strong community of black women emerges; when this unified front breaks down, the women are left defenseless, and a tragedy occurs. Home, the friendships of women, and the power of community are important themes in the novel. Furthermore, by focusing on a diverse cast of characters, Naylor also examines notions of sexuality, motherhood, and masculinity.

Friendship among Women

The men in the novel—husbands, fathers, and sons—abandon or abuse the women, who turn to one another for support and love. Naylor depicts women's love as unconditional and long lasting, such as the relationship between Mattie and Etta. Their friendship saves them from despair and loneliness. After Etta's night with the reverend, she feels tired and lonely, until she sees that Mattie is waiting up. Willingly, she "climbed the steps toward the light and the love and the comfort that awaited her."

The novel is a celebration of women, and by focusing on the bonds connecting them, Naylor shows how a community can offer protection, love, and a sense of home. When Ciel wants to die, it is Mattie's touch that brings her back to the land of the living, a scene that symbolizes the healing power of women. However, when the women fail to extend their friendship to Theresa and Lorraine, Lorraine is abandoned, a turn of events that results in tragedy and a breakdown of the entire community. Mattie at one point struggles to understand the women's sexuality, and at first she feels uncomfortable. Later she decides that the love and mutual support that unite her and Etta are possibly "not so different." Mattie admits to Etta that she has loved some women "deeper than I ever loved a man." Etta and Mattie share a strong, platonic love, reflecting the intimacy that Theresa and Lorraine share. In the end, Mattie is there to hold the dying Lorraine in her arms. She dreams of the community coming together and putting the pain of the past behind them; the ending, with the sun shining, seems to imply such a possibility.

The Meaning of Home

Many of the women are in search of a home, whether it is a physical or spiritual place they seek. Some of Mattie's strongest memories are of her childhood home, and after she leaves with her baby, she searches for a new place to live. When Miss Eva takes her in, she finds a real home—a nurturing, warm, harmonious place where she stays for 30 years; this also begins her commitment to being in the company of women. Although Brewster Place is run down and ugly, the women who inhabit it create a nurturing space, and Mattie and the others consider it home. Home is a state of mind, dependent on the people who live there. Etta, restless and ever in motion, considers Brewster Place her home because there she has a true friend waiting up for her. Kiswana chooses to engage the community around her and to be with "her people," a transformation that, in the end, helps her to understand where she comes from. Only Theresa and Lorraine, who are looking for a place where they will be accepted, are not integrated or welcomed into the community. Naylor, in revolving each of her stories around the central location of Brewster Place, portrays how home is not necessarily a building or a physical space but found in the people who inhabit it instead.

CHRONOLOGY

1928
- Maya Angelou born as Marguerite Johnson on April 4 in St. Louis, Missouri, to Bailey and Vivian Baxter Johnson.

1931
- Toni Morrison born as Chloe Anthony Wofford on February 18 in Lorain, Ohio, to George and Ramah (Willis) Wofford.

1933
- Ernest J. Gaines born on January 15 to Manuel and Adrienne Gaines in Pointe Coupee Parish, Louisiana.

1937
- Walter Dean Myers is born Walter Milton Myers on August 12 in Martinsburg, West Virginia.
- Zora Neale Hurston's *Their Eyes Were Watching God* published.

1940
- Richard Wright's *Native Son* published.

1944
- Alice Walker born on February 9, in Eatonton, Georgia, the youngest of eight children, to Willie Lee Walker and Minnie Tallulah.

1945
- August Wilson is born Frederick August Kittel on April 27 in Pittsburgh's Hill District to Frederick Kittel and Daisy Wilson.

- Richard Wright's *Black Boy* published.

1947
- Jackie Robinson of the Brooklyn Dodgers becomes the first African American to play Major League Baseball in the twentieth century.

1948
- Charles Johnson born April 23 in Evanston, Illinois, to Benny Lee Johnson and Ruby Elizabeth Johnson.

1950
- Gloria Naylor born in New York City on January 25 to Roosevelt and Alberta McAlpin Naylor.
- Poet Gwendolyn Brooks of Chicago becomes the first African American to receive a Pulitzer Prize.

1951
- Langston Hughes publishes *Montage of a Dream Deferred*.

1952
- Ralph Ellison publishes *Invisible Man*.

1954
- In *Brown v. Board of Education*, the Supreme Court declares segregation in schools unconstitutional.

1955
- James Baldwin publishes *Notes of a Native Son*.
- 14-year-old Emmett Till lynched in Mississippi.
- Rosa Parks arrested for refusing to give seat on bus to white man, setting off a bus boycott led by Martin Luther King Jr.

1957
- Congress passes the Civil Rights Act of 1957, the first legislation protecting black rights since Reconstruction.
- President Eisenhower sends federal troops to Little Rock, Arkansas, to ensure the enforcement of a federal court order to desegregate Central High School and to protect nine African-American students.

1959
- Paule Marshall's novel *Brown Girl, Brownstones* published.
- Lorraine Hansberry's *A Raisin in the Sun* is the first Broadway play by an African-American woman.

1961

- The Congress of Racial Equality organizes Freedom Rides through parts of the South.

1963

- Martin Luther King's *Letter from Birmingham Jail* published.
- The March on Washington, where King delivers his "I Have a Dream" speech, attracts more than 200,000 demonstrators.
- President Kennedy assassinated on November 22.
- James Baldwin publishes *The Fire Next Time*.

1964

- Ernest Gaines publishes his first novel, *Catherine Carmier*.
- Martin Luther King wins the Nobel Peace Prize.
- Congress passes the Economic Opportunity Act and the Civil Rights Act of 1964, which bans discrimination in all public accommodations and by employers.

1965-73

- The Vietnam War.

1965

- *The Autobiography of Malcolm X* by Alex Haley published.
- Malcolm X is assassinated in New York City on February 21.
- Black Arts movement is started by Amiri Baraka in Harlem.

1966

- Black Panthers founded.

1967

- Ernest Gaines's *Of Love and Dust* published.
- Thurgood Marshall becomes first black U.S. Supreme Court justice.

1968

- Martin Luther King Jr. is assassinated on April 4.
- Alice Walker publishes her first book, *Once*, a volume of poetry.
- Walter Dean Myers's first book, a picture book titled *Where Does the Day Go?*, wins first prize in a writing contest sponsored by the Council on Interracial Books for Children.
- Ernest Gaines's *Bloodline* is published.

1970

- Toni Morrison's *The Bluest Eye* published.
- Maya Angelou's *I Know Why the Caged Bird Sings* nominated for a National Book Award.
- Alice Walker publishes her first novel, *The Third Life of Grange Copeland*.

1971
- Maya Angelou's collection of poetry *Just Give Me a Cool Drink of Water 'Fore I Diiie* is nominated for a Pulitzer Prize.
- Ernest Gaines publishes *A Long Day in November* and *The Autobiography of Miss Jane Pittman*.

1973
- Toni Morrison's *Sula*, her second novel, is published.
- Alice Walker publishes *In Love and Trouble: Stories of Black Women* and *Revolutionary Petunias and Other Poems*.

1974
- Maya Angelou's *Gather Together in My Name* is published.
- Charles Johnson publishes *Faith and the Good Thing*, his first novel.

1975
- Maya Angelou's *Oh Pray My Wings Are Gonna Fit Me Well* is published.
- Walter Dean Myers's first young-adult novel, *Fast Sam, Cool Clyde, and Stuff*, is published.
- Ntozake Shange's *for colored girls who have considered suicide / when the rainbow is enuf* is produced on Broadway.

1976
- Maya Angelou's *Singin' and Swingin' and Gettin' Merry Like Christmas* is published
- Alice Walker's novel *Meridian* published.

1977
- Toni Morrison's *Song of Solomon* published. It is a Book-of-the-Month Club selection, the first by an African-American author since Richard Wright's *Native Son*. Receives National Book Critics Circle Award and the American Academy and Institute of Arts and Letters Award.
- The television miniseries based on Alex Haley's *Roots* attracts more viewers than any television program in history.

1978
- Maya Angelou's *And I Still Rise* is published.
- Ernest Gaines publishes *In My Father's House*.

1979
- Alice Walker publishes a collection of poetry, *Goodnight, Willie Lee, I'll See You in the Morning*, and *I Love Myself When I'm Laughing: A Zora Neale Hurston Reader*.
- Toni Cade Bambara's *The Salt Eaters* wins the American Book Award.

1981
- Toni Morrison's *Tar Baby* is published.

- Maya Angelou's *The Heart of a Woman* is published.
- Alice Walker's *You Can't Keep a Good Woman Down* published.
- Walter Dean Myers's *Hoops* published.

1982

- Gloria Naylor publishes *The Women of Brewster Place*, which receives the American Book Award for best first novel.
- Charles Johnson's *Oxherding Tale* is published.
- August Wilson's *Jitney* staged by Allegheny Repertory Theatre in Pittsburgh.

1983

- Maya Angelou publishes *Shaker, Why Don't you Sing?*
- Ernest Gaines publishes *A Gathering of Old Men.*
- Alice Walker's *The Color Purple* (1982) receives the Pulitzer Prize for Fiction and the American Book Award. *In Search of Our Mothers' Gardens: Womanist Prose* published.

1984

- August Wilson's *Ma Rainey's Black Bottom* premieres at the Yale Repertory Theatre and then moves to Broadway; wins the New York Drama Critics' Circle Award for Best Play of the Year.

1985

- August Wilson's *Fences* premieres at the Yale Repertory Theatre.
- Gloria Naylor publishes *Linden Hills.*
- Walter Dean Myers receives the Coretta Scott King Award for *Motown and Didi: A Love Story.*
- Alice Walker's *Horses Make a Landscape Look More Beautiful* published.

1986

- August Wilson's *Joe Turner's Come and Gone* premieres at the Yale Repertory Theatre.
- Maya Angelou publishes *All God's Children Need Traveling Shoes* and *Poems: Maya Angelou.*
- The film *The Color Purple* receives 11 Academy Award nominations but wins no Oscars.
- Charles Johnson's *The Sorcerer's Apprentice*, a collection of short stories, is published.

1987

- August Wilson's *Fences* opens on Broadway; earns Wilson a Tony Award for best play as well as Pulitzer Prize for Drama.
- Rita Dove wins the Pulitzer Prize for Poetry.

1988

- Toni Morrison's *Beloved* (1987) receives the Pulitzer Prize for Fiction.
- Gloria Naylor publishes *Mama Day.*
- August Wilson's *Joe Turner's Come and Gone* opens on Broadway.

- Alice Walker publishes *Living by the Word: Selected Writings 1973–1986* and *To Hell with Dying.*

1989
- Walter Dean Myers receives Coretta Scott King Award for *Fallen Angels; Scorpions* is chosen as a Newbery Honor Book.
- Alice Walker publishes *Temple of My Familiar.*

1990
- Maya Angelou publishes a collection of poems, *I Shall Not Be Moved.*
- August Wilson's *Two Trains Running* premieres at the Yale Repertory Theatre, and *The Piano Lesson* opens on Broadway; earns Wilson his second Pulitzer Prize for Drama.
- Charles Johnson's *Middle Passage* wins a National Book Award.

1991
- Alice Walker publishes *Her Blue Body Everything We Know: Earthling Poems 1965–1990*

1992
- *Jazz*, Toni Morrison's sixth novel, published. Also publishes *Playing in the Dark: Essays on Whiteness and the Literary Imagination* and edits *Race-ing Justice, En-Gendering Power: Essays on Anita Hill, Clarence Thomas and the Construction of Social Reality.*
- Gloria Naylor's *Bailey's Café* published.
- August Wilson's *Two Trains Running* opens at the Walter Kerr Theatre on Broadway.
- Alice Walker's *Possessing the Secret of Joy* published.
- *Waiting to Exhale* by Terry McMillan published.

1993
- Toni Morrison wins Nobel Prize in Literature, the first African American to win.
- Maya Angelou recites her poem "On the Pulse of Morning" at President Bill Clinton's inauguration, the first poet to read at an inauguration since Robert Frost at John F. Kennedy's inauguration in 1961.
- Ernest Gaines's *A Lesson Before Dying* wins the National Book Critics Circle Award for fiction; Gaines wins MacArthur Fellowship.
- Charles Johnson wins O. Henry Prize for "Kwoon," a short story.
- Alice Walker publishes *Warrior Marks: Female Genital Mutilation and the Sexual Blindness of Women* and releases film by same title.
- Rita Dove named U.S. poet laureate.

1995
- Toni Morrison receives a National Book Award for lifetime achievement.
- August Wilson's *Seven Guitars* opens on Broadway.
- The Million Man March in Washington, D.C., organized by Nation of Islam minister Louis Farrakhan.
- Walter Dean Myers's *The Glory Field* published.

1996
- August Wilson's *Seven Guitars* premieres on Broadway at the Walter Kerr Theatre.

1997
- Maya Angelou's *Even the Stars Look Lonesome* published.
- Charles Johnson co-edits *Black Men Speaking*, an anthology of literature about the experience of African-American males.
- Walter Dean Myers's *Somewhere in the Darkness* published; *Hoops* wins Coretta Scott King Author Award.

1998
- Gloria Naylor's *The Men of Brewster Place* published.
- Toni Morrison's *Paradise* published.
- Alice Walker publishes *By the Light of My Father's Smile*, a novel.
- Charles Johnson is awarded a MacArthur Fellowship; publishes *Dreamer*.

1999
- August Wilson's *Jitney* debuts at Baltimore's Centerstage Theatre.
- Walter Dean Myers's *Monster* is published, wins Coretta Scott King Author Award the following year.

2000
- Charles Johnson publishes *Soulcatcher*.

2001
- August Wilson's *King Hedley II* opens at the Virginia Theatre on Broadway.

2002
- Maya Angelou's *A Song Flung Up to Heaven* published.

2003
- Toni Morrison's *Love* published.
- Charles Johnson publishes a collection of essays, *Turning the Wheel*.
- Alice Walker's *A Poem Traveled Down My Arm: Poems and Drawings* and *Absolute Trust in the Goodness of the Earth* published.

2004
- *The Collected Autobiographies of Maya Angelou* published.
- Walter Dean Myers's *Shooter* is published.
- August Wilson's *Gem of the Ocean* opens at the Walter Kerr Theatre on Broadway.
- Edward Jones wins the Pulitzer Prize for Fiction for his novel *The Known World*.

2005

- August Wilson's *Radio Golf* premieres at the Yale Repertory Theatre, completing his 10-play cycle. He is diagnosed with liver cancer and dies on October 2 at the age of 60.
- Gloria Naylor publishes *1996*.
- Ernest Gaines publishes *Mozart and Leadbelly: Stories and Essays*.
- Walter Dean Myers's *Autobiography of My Dead Brother* published.

2007

- Walter Dean Myers's *What They Found: Love on 145 Street* is published.

2008

- Toni Morrison's *A Mercy* published.

ADDITIONAL READING

The Autobiography of Malcolm X by Malcolm X and Alex Haley

A landmark of twentieth-century American nonfiction, this memoir was constructed by Haley after a series of conversations with the controversial black Muslim and civil rights leader Malcolm X. The work chronicles his coming of age, time spent in prison, conversion to the Nation of Islam, and emergence as an often radical commentator on the state of race and race relations in the United States during and leading up to the civil rights era.

Black Boy by Richard Wright

This 1945 autobiography gives voice to Wright's uneasy relationship not only to the racist agenda of white southern society but to the family members and black community that reared him. In this coming-of-age memoir, Wright struggles to find his voice, as an author and as an individual, in a restrictive and oppressive world he struggles to break free of in the less confining cities of the North.

Breath, Eyes, Memory by Edwidge Danticat

Published in 1994 when the author was twenty-five years old, this novel takes up themes of gender and racial equality in presenting the coming of age of a young Haitian woman who immigrates to the United States.

A Gathering of Old Men by Ernest Gaines

Set in the 1970s on a Louisiana sugarcane plantation, the novel is a powerful depiction of racial tensions. After a Cajun man is found dead, 18 old black men, armed with shotguns, all claim to have killed him. They band together against the whites who seek vengeance for the man's murder.

Go Tell It on the Mountain by James Baldwin

This semiautobiographical novel from 1953 centers on the origins and coming of age of a frail and awkward adolescent. While Baldwin interweaves themes of the destructive patterns of racism into the work, his primary focus is on the effects of the church in the lives of African Americans, offering them hope, support, and community, while at the same time existing as a source of moral hypocrisy and repression.

The Intuitionist by Colson Whitehead

Using the world of elevator inspection as a metaphor for self-advancement and racial progress in the United States, Whitehead's 1999 novel centers on Lila Mae Watson, an unnamed city's first black female elevator inspector who discovers the principles behind the perfect elevator, one that leads to an idealized city of the future.

Invisible Man by Ralph Ellison

Hailed as one of the most accomplished American novels of the century, Ellison's work from 1952 follows a nameless protagonist invisible, because of his skin color, to the inhabitants of the world around him. Ellison uses his premise to explore issues of individuality and black nationalism and identity.

Joe Turner's Come and Gone by August Wilson

The second installment, chronologically, in Wilson's Pittsburgh Cycle, the play is set in the second decade of the twentieth century and chronicles the struggles of individuals and families attempting to emerge from the shadow of slavery and reconstruct their lives and legacies in the North. The drama centers on themes of identity, migration, and reconstruction, as embodied in the lives of the residents of Seth Holly's boardinghouse.

The Known World by Edward Jones

Awarded the Pulitzer Prize for fiction in 2004, the novel dramatizes a little known and less common reality in the pre–Civil War South: slaves owned by black slaveholders. The rich cast of characters lend their various voices to Jones's appraisal of the ways slavery negates human identity.

Native Son by Richard Wright

Wright's 1940 protest novel tells the story of 20-year-old Bigger Thomas. Through its naturalistic details and dramatization of the conflict between societal conditioning and the exercise of individual will, Wright presents a flawed protagonist who, in the face of racism and debasement, succumbs to violence and crime.

Push by Sapphire

This 1996 novel centers on Claireece "Precious" Jones, a 16-year-old Harlem resident who has known only a life of poverty and physical and sexual abuse. Narrated by Precious in a stream-of-consciousness style, the novel vibrantly gives life to an urban teenager struggling to rise above the harsh conditions of her existence.

A Raisin in the Sun by Lorraine Hansberry

This breakthrough drama was the first play written by a black author to be produced on the Broadway stage. It tells the story of the Youngers, a family that does not allow its dreams of a better life, and a new house in an otherwise all-white neighborhood, to be thwarted by the racist and segregationist attitudes that dominated post–World War II America.

A Soldier's Play by Charles Fuller

This Pulitzer Prize–winning drama uses the murder mystery formula as a means of exploring the ways some blacks, in this case soldiers stationed in racially segregated Louisiana in 1944, absorbed white racist attitudes, directing their hatred and resentment at one another. An army officer investigates the murder of Sergeant Vernon Waters, a black man haunted by self-hatred and disdain for the black world in which he was raised.

Song of Solomon by Toni Morrison

This magical novel follows the life of Macon "Milkman" Dead III, an African-American male living in Michigan, who was born shortly after a neighborhood eccentric hurled himself off a rooftop in an attempt to fly. The novel follows Milkman on his quest for his identity, as he tries to piece together the history of his ancestors. Morrison examines four generations of black life in the United States, interweaving their respective viewpoints while creating a rich cast of characters.

Their Eyes Were Watching God by Zora Neale Hurston

Once overlooked if not long forgotten, this classic work was rediscovered through the efforts of Alice Walker and is now considered a watershed work in the history of African-American literature. Hinging on the life of Janie Crawford, Hurston's novel is known for its dialect-inflected dialogue and for its portrait of a powerful female protagonist who resists the confining categories community and society force her to inhabit.

BIBLIOGRAPHY

Books

Abernathy, Jeff. *To Hell and Back: Race and Betrayal in the Southern Novel*. Athens: University of Georgia Press, 2003.

Andrews, William L. and Nellie Y. McKay, eds. *Toni Morrison's Beloved: A Casebook*. New York: Oxford University Press, 1999.

Auger, Philip. *Native Sons in No Man's Land: Rewriting Afro-American Manhood in the Novels of Baldwin, Walker, Wideman, and Gaines*. New York: Garland Pub., 2000.

Awkward, Michael. *Inspiring Influences: Tradition, Revision, and Afro-American Women's Novels*. New York: Columbia UP, 1991.

Barker, E. Ellen. "Creating Generations: The Relationship Between Celie and Shug in Alice Walker's The Color Purple." *Critical Essays on Alice Walker*. Ikenna Dieke, ed. Westport, CT: Greenwood Press, 1999. 45–54.

Berlant, Lauren. "Race, Gender, and Nation in The Color Purple." In *Alice Walker: Critical Perspectives Past and Present*. Henry Louis Gates Jr. and K.A. Appiah, eds. New York: Amistad Press, 1993. 211–238.

Bevers, Herman. *Wrestling Angels into Song: The Fictions of Ernest J. Gaines and James Alan McPherson*. Philadelphia; University of Pennsylvania Press, 1995.

Bigsby, Christopher, ed. *The Cambridge Companion to August Wilson*. Cambridge: Cambridge University Press, 2007.

Bishop, Rudine Sims. *Presenting Walter Dean Myers*. Boston: Twayne Publishers, 1991.

Boccia, Michael and Herman Beavers, eds. "Charles Johnson Issue." *African American Review* 30, no. 4 (1996).

Booker, Margaret. *Lillian Hellman and August Wilson: Dramatizing a New American Identity*. NY: Peter Lang, 2003.

Braxton, Joanne M. "A Song of Transcendence: Maya Angelou." In *Black Women Writing Autobiography*. Philadelphia: Temple University, 1989. 181–201.

Burshtein, Karen. *Walter Dean Myers*. New York: Rosen Publishing Group, 2004.

Butler-Evans, Elliott. *Race, Gender, and Desire: Narrative Strategies in the Fiction of Toni Cade Bambara, Toni Morrison, and Alice Walker*. Philadelphia; Temple University Press, 1989.

Byrd, Rudolph P. *Charles Johnson's Novels: Writing the American Palimpsest*. Bloomington: Indiana University Press, 2005.

Christian, Barbara. *Black Feminist Criticism: Perspectives on Black Women Writers*. New York: Pergamon, 1985.

Clark, Keith. *Black Manhood in James Baldwin, Ernest J. Gaines and August Wilson*. Urbana: U of Illinois P, 2002.

Dieke, Ikenna. *Critical Essays on Alice Walker*. Westport, CT: Greenwood Press, 1999.

Doyle, Mary E. *Voices from the Quarters: The Fiction of Ernest J. Gaines*. Baton Rouge: Louisiana State UP, 2002.

Elam, Harry J., Jr. *The Past as Present in the Drama of August Wilson*. Ann Arbor, MI: University of Michigan Press, 2004.

Elkins, Marilyn. ed. *August Wilson: A Casebook*. NY: Garland, 2000.

Estes, David C., ed. *Critical Reflections on the Fiction of Ernest J. Gaines*. Athens: University of Georgia Press, 1994.

Evans, Mari, ed. *Black Women Writers (1950–1980): A Critical Evaluation*. Garden City, NY: Anchor-Doubleday, 1984.

Felton, Sharon and Michelle Loris, eds. *Naylor: The Critical Response to Gloria Naylor*. Westport: Greenwood Press, 1997.

Fowler, Virginia. *Gloria Naylor: In Search of Sanctuary*. New York: Twayne Publishers 1996.

Gates, Henry Louis. *The Signifying Monkey: A Theory of Afro-American Literary Criticism*. New York: Oxford University Press, 1988.

——— and Alan Nadel. eds. *May All Your Fences Have Gates: Essays on the Drama of August Wilson*. U of Iowa, 1993.

——— and K.A. Appiah, eds. *Alice Walker: Critical Perspectives Past and Present*. Amistad Press: New York, 1993.

———, eds. *Gloria Naylor: Critical Perspectives Past and Present*. New York: Amistad Press Inc. 1993.

———, eds. *Toni Morrison: Critical Perspectives Past and Present*. New York: Amistad, 1993.

Hagen, Lyman B. *Heart of a Woman, Mind of a Writer, and Soul of a Poet: A Critical Analysis of the Writings of Maya Angelou*. Lanham, MD: University Press of America, 1997.

Harris, Trudier. *Fiction and Folklore: The Novels of Toni Morrison*. Knoxville: University of Tennessee Press, 1991.

——— . "On *The Color Purple*, Stereotypes and Silence." *Black American Literature Forum* 18 (Winter 1984): 155–161.

——— . *The Power of the Porch: The Storyteller's Craft in Zora Neale Hurston, Gloria Naylor, and Randall Kenan*. Athens: University of Georgia Press, 1996.

hooks, bell. In *Alice Walker: Critical Perspectives Past and Present*. "Reading and Resistance: The Color Purple." New York: Amistad Press, 1993. 296–308.

Howard, Lillie P. ed. *Alice Walker and Zora Neale Hurston: The Common Bond*. Westport, CT: Greenwood, 1993.

Ikard, David. *Breaking the Silence: Toward a Black Male Feminist Criticism*. Baton Rouge: Louisiana State University Press, 2007.

Kelley, Margot Anne, ed. *Gloria Naylor's Early Novels*. Gainesville: University Press of Florida, 1999.

King, Lovalerie and Lynn Orilla Scott, eds. *James Baldwin and Toni Morrison: Comparative Critical and Theoretical Essays*. New York: Palgrave MacMillan, 2006.

Kolmerten, Carol A., Stephen M. Ross and Judith Bryant Wittenberg, eds. *Unflinching Gaze: Morrison and Faulkner Re-envisioned*. Jackson: University of Mississippi, 1997.

Little, Jonathan. *Charles Johnson's Spiritual Imagination*. Columbia: University of Missouri Press, 1997.

Lowe, John, ed. *Conversations with Ernest Gaines*. Jackson: University Press of Mississippi, 1995.

Lupton, Mary Jane. *Maya Angelou: A Critical Companion*. Westport, CT: Greenwood Press, 1998.

McPherson, Dolly A. "Initiation and Self-Discovery." From *Maya Angelou's I Know Why The Caged Bird Sings: A Casebook*. Joanne M. Braxton, ed. New York: Oxford University Press, 1999.

McWilliams, Jim, ed. *Passing the Three Gates: Interviews with Charles Johnson*. Seattle: University of Washington Press, 2004.

Montgomery, Lavon Maxine. *Conversations with Gloria Naylor*. Jackson: University Press of Mississippi, 2004.

Nash, William R. *Charles Johnson's Fiction*. Champaign: University of Illinois Press, 2002.

O'Keefe, Vincent A. "Reading Rigor Mortis: Offstage Violence and Excluded Middles in Johnson's *Middle Passage* and Morrison's *Beloved*." *African American Review* 30.4 (1996): 635–646.

Pereira, Kim. *August Wilson & the African-American Odyssey*. University of Illinois Press, 1995.

Peterson, Nancy J. and John N. Duvall, eds. *Toni Morrison Special Issue. MFS: Modern Fiction Studies* 52, no. 2 (Summer 2006).

Rushdy, Ashraf H.A. *Neo-slave Narratives: Studies in the Social Logic of a Literary Form*. New York: Oxford University Press, 1999.

Shannon, Sandra G. *The Dramatic Vision of August Wilson*. Washington, DC: Howard UP, 1996.

Showalter, Elaine. "Piecing and Writing." *The Poetics of Gender*. Nancy K. Miller, Ed. New York: Columbia UP, 1986. 222–247.

Snodgrass, Mary Ellen, *Walter Dean Myers: A Literary Companion*. Jefferson, NC: McFarland & Co., 2006.

Spillers, Hortense J. ed. *Comparative American Identities: Race, Sex, and Nationality in the Modern Text*. New York: Routledge, 1991. 62–86.

Storhoff, Gary. *Understanding Charles Johnson*. Columbia: University of South Carolina Press, 2004.

Tate, Claudia, ed. "Alice Walker." In *Black Women Writers at Work*. New York: Continuum, 1983.

Travis, Molly Abel. "*Beloved and Middle Passage*: Race, Narrative, and the Critic's Essentialism." *Narrative* 2.3 (1994): 179–200.

Vermillion, Mary. "Reembodying the Self: Representations of Rape in *Incidents in the Life of a Slave Girl* and *I Know Why the Caged Bird Sings.*" *Biography: An Interdisciplinary Quarterly* 15, no. 3 (Summer 1992): 243–260.

Wall, Cheryl A. *Worrying the Line: Black Women Writers, Lineage, and Literary Tradition.* Chapel Hill: University of North Carolina Press, 2005.

Ward, Kathleen L. *From a Position of Strength: Black Women Writing in the Eighties,* 1993.

Wolf, Peter. *August Wilson.* NY: Twayne Publishers, 1999.

Websites

Academy of Achievement: Maya Angelou
http://www.achievement.org/autodoc/page/ang0bio-1

African American Literature Book Club: Alice Walker
http://aalbc.com/authors/alice.htm

African American Literature Book Club: Ernest Gaines
http://aalbc.com/authors/ernest.htm

African American Authors: A Celebration
http://www.mtsu.edu/~vvesper/afam.html

African American World Timeline: PBS
http://www.pbs.org/wnet/aaworld/timeline.html

Charles Johnson Website
http://www.oxherdingtale.com/

The Charles Johnson Society
http://charlesjohnson.wlu.edu/

Contemporary Theatre and Drama in the U.S.: August Wilson
http://www.fb10.uni-bremen.de/anglistik/kerkhoff/ContempDrama/
WilsonAugust.htm

Homepage for August Wilson
http://www.augustwilson.net/

Maya Angelou Official Website
http://www.mayaangelou.com/

The New Georgia Encyclopedia: Alice Walker
http://www.georgiaencyclopedia.org/nge/Article.jsp?id=h-998

Nobel Prize: Toni Morrison
http://nobelprize.org/nobel_prizes/literature/laureates/1993/

Official Website of the Toni Morrison Society
http://www.tonimorrisonsociety.org/

PAL: Ernest Gaines
http://www.csustan.edu/english/reuben/pal/chap10/gaines.html

Voices from the Gaps: Gloria Naylor
http://voices.cla.umn.edu/vg/Bios/entries/naylor_gloria.html

Voices from the Gaps: Toni Morrison
http://voices.cla.umn.edu/vg/Bios/entries/morrison_toni.html

Walter Dean Myers Website
http://www.walterdeanmyers.net/

Website of Teenreads.com: Walter Dean Myers
http://www.teenreads.com/authors/au-myers-walterdean.asp

Wikipedia: Gloria Naylor
http://en.wikipedia.org/wiki/Gloria_Naylor

PICTURE CREDITS

Page

INDEX